Strategies for Success

STRATEGIES FOR SUCCESS

Classroom Teaching Techniques for Students with Learning Problems

Lynn J. Meltzer
Bethany N. Roditi
Donna P. Haynes
Kathleen Rafter Biddle
Michelle Paster
Susan E. Taber

Illustrations by Anthony L. Ciccarelli

pro·ed
An International Publisher

8700 Shoal Creek Boulevard, Austin, Texas 78757-6897

An International Publisher

© 1996 by PRO-ED, Inc.
8700 Shoal Creek Boulevard
Austin, Texas 78757-6897

Library of Congress Cataloging-in-Publication Data

Strategies for success : classroom teaching techniques for students
    with learning problems / Lynn Meltzer ... [et al.].
        p.   cm.
    "Revised December 1994."
    Includes bibliographical references (p.).
    ISBN 0-89079-673-4 (spiralbound)
        1. Learning disabled children—Education.   2. Teaching.
    I. Meltzer, Lynn.
LC4704.S767   1995
371.9—dc20   95-18217
                                                       CIP

This book is designed in Stone Serif and Univers Ultra Condensed.

Production Manager: Alan Grimes
Production Coordinator: Karen Swain
Managing Editor: Tracy Sergo
Art Director: Thomas Barkley
Reprints Buyer: Alicia Woods
Editor: Marilyn Novell
Editorial Assistant: Claudette Landry
Editorial Assistant: Martin Wilson

Printed in the United States of America

3   4   5   6   7   8   9   10   00   99   98

We would like to thank

Ronald McDonald Children's Charities

for funding and supporting this project to enrich the classroom learning of all children, and particularly children with special learning needs.

Contents

Acknowledgments

We would like to thank the staff at Resear*chILD* and the Institute for Learning and Development for their suggestions, help, and encouragement.

We are particularly grateful to Beth Rudin, MEd, for developing many original graphic organizers, for her invaluable ideas, and for her generous support in editing.

A special thanks to Enid Wetzner, MA, for developing a number of the case studies and for her organizational expertise and editing help.

Thanks, too, to Judith Stein, PhD, Susan Nadeau, MEd, Robin Rogers-Brown, MEd, Kalyani Krishnan, MA, and Rebecca Schachne, BA, for their suggestions and editing help.

We are especially thankful to Linda Green, MEd, for her encouragement and support throughout the many stages of the preparation of this book.

Finally, this book could not have been produced without the hard work and dedication of Thelma Segal and Angela Cunha, who carefully typed and corrected the many versions of the manuscript.

Preface

I feel like a bottle of ginger ale—I need the fizzle to settle before I can do what I need to do." (Chris, age 11 years)

"I can't spell good and my mind has all these ideas and so it comes out looking wrong, so I erase and then I have to start over again and then I forget the ideas." (Ben, age 9 years)

Children like Chris and Ben are spending more and more time in the regular classroom rather than in special education settings. For regular classroom teachers, students like these are difficult to understand because of the inconsistencies in their performance in reasoning, problem solving, and basic skills. How can we help teachers to modify classroom expectations and teaching techniques to encourage positive learning experiences and insure academic success for students like Chris and Ben?

In this manual we provide classroom teaching strategies that can be easily implemented in a cost-effective fashion. *Strategies for Success* consists of realistic and accessible teaching methods for teachers, special educators, and other professionals working with students at the late elementary, middle, and early high school levels. These specific strategies can help teachers develop a better understanding of the diverse learning profiles of their students, allowing them to create a classroom environment that encourages all their students to succeed. This academic success can often break the negative cycle of failure experienced by students like Chris and Ben, thus reducing their feelings of vulnerability and helplessness.

The importance and timeliness of this manual are highlighted by recent changes in the special education laws, which have resulted in the inclusion of special needs students in the regular classroom setting. This mainstreaming initiative or inclusion model, termed the Regular Education Initiative (REI), was designed to reduce the stigma that results when special needs students are separated from their peers for instructional purposes. Implementation of the inclusion model so far has been difficult, because regular classroom teachers require additional training to understand and teach students with diverse learning profiles. Many dedicated and excellent teachers have felt overwhelmed by requests to individualize their programs to meet the specific needs of students in their classrooms. We hope that these teachers will benefit from the contents of this handbook, including specific classroom accommodations, teaching strategies, and bypass techniques for addressing the unique needs of students in heterogeneous classes.

Distribution of a preliminary draft of *Strategies for Success* to selected teachers elicited many enthusiastic comments, including the following:

> I wish to extend a vote of thanks on behalf of all educators for collating this useful information for enhancing teaching practices. All teachers who contribute to the positive development of learners should find that this manual is user-friendly, informative and "sets the tone" for sound practices in the classroom.

> This manual is a a terrific tool for teachers. It supplies them with very important strategies and information that can be extremely useful in their classrooms working with all students, not just LD and ADD students.

We hope that all teachers will find this manual as helpful as did our teacher reviewers and that implementation of these strategies will reduce the frustration of teachers as well as students. We also hope that the strategies contained in this manual will stimulate teachers to share some of their own strategies with us so that we can create an expanding data bank of strategies for use by all teachers.

Section I

The Importance of Learning Strategies

Chapter 1

Strategic Learning in the Classroom

Approximately 5% to 10% of all schoolchildren display poor academic performance despite average to above average intelligence. These children may manifest specific delays in language-based skills, especially reading and writing, and may also be formally classified as having learning disabilities and/or attention deficit disorders. These students present a major challenge for teachers because they often show remarkable talents in areas that require reasoning and problem solving, yet struggle with rote skills such as memorization of multiplication tables and spelling. They may obtain excellent grades on classroom assignments, yet fail in more formal test situations. Because the majority of these students are now integrated into regular classrooms, every teacher must deal with the challenge of instructing children who learn differently. Furthermore, because each student has a unique learning style, teachers are required to address a broad range of learning needs.

Strategies for Success provides answers to the following questions:

- How can teaching techniques be modified to insure stimulation for all students during the learning process, while simultaneously teaching the skills essential for meeting the challenges of higher level conceptual tasks?

- How can classroom teachers address the broad range of students' learning profiles in view of the practical constraints of the school setting, such as limited planning time, reduced budgets, and few opportunities for teacher training?

- How can we help all students to maximize their strengths and to achieve their potential?

- How can classroom expectations and teaching techniques be developed to enrich the learning of all students in the classroom?

- How can we prevent students from experiencing ongoing failure and long-term frustration, which can often lead to a negative cycle of behavioral and social problems?

The purpose of this manual is to help teachers better understand the learning profiles of their students and to insure that all students experience success, mastery, and achievement in the classroom. We hope this manual will help teachers to create classroom environments that encourage all students to display their strengths and compensate for their weaknesses. Minor modifications in teaching can often provide the opportunities for students to realize their academic and social potential, while simultaneously alleviating a great deal of misery and unnecessary frustration. Academic success can reduce students' feelings of vulnerability and helplessness and can break the negative cycle of failure so often experienced.

Why Learning Strategies Should Be Taught

Terms such as *learning strategies, teaching strategies,* and *strategic learning* are now widely used to imply that learners can choose specific procedures for accomplishing particular tasks. These strategies can help students improve their reading, writing, math, and problem-solving performance. The importance of strategic learning has been demonstrated in work showing that successful learners use effective strategies to process information (Brown & Campione, 1986; Harris & Graham, 1992; Meltzer, 1993a; Palincsar, Winn, David, Snyder, & Stevens, 1993; Pressley, Goodchild, Fleet, Zajchowski, & Evans, 1989). In contrast, students with learning difficulties often show weaknesses in strategic learning that may affect their performance in a broad range of content areas and may mask their many strengths (Meltzer, 1993a, 1993b; Swanson, 1991). These students may process information differently from other students, they may use different routes to access information, and they may not use appropriate strategies to improve their efficiency and accuracy.

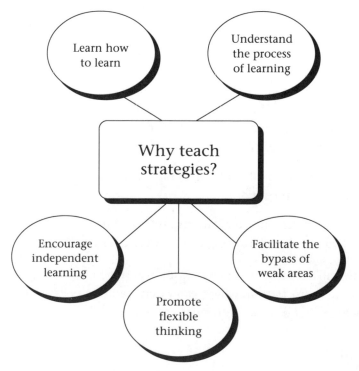

The how and why of students' processing styles are often submerged in the end products of learning as reflected in students' oral and written answers. Therefore, an appropriate understanding of a student's repertoire of strategies is an important precursor to teaching. Students' learning profiles differ as do teaching styles, making an appropriate teacher–student match critical. This match is particularly important for students with learning difficulties, who may use different processing routes to achieve their goals and need teachers whose styles can accommodate their diversity. These students often become more effective as learners when they acquire learning strategies that help them reach the goals of learning more efficiently. Learning strategies emphasize the process of learning and help students learn how to learn. As students learn to think flexibly, they are able to rely on their strengths in order to bypass their weaknesses, thereby becoming more independent and efficient as learners.

Students with learning difficulties are often inefficient as learners because they have difficulty prioritizing and identifying major themes. They frequently overfocus on details and show major organizational difficulties, which affects their rate and efficiency as learners. Although they may reach the same goals as their normally achieving peers, they often differ in how they get there, how fast they get there, and the frustration they experience en route. Just as a roundabout route to a destination may be frustrating because it is very time-consuming, so learning may be frustrating when the process is long and arduous and the goal is not easily visible.

Can Strategies Be Taught?

Strategies can be taught in a structured and systematic way. In the classroom setting, explicit strategy instruction is beneficial for all students, but it is essential for students with learning difficulties. Students with learning difficulties need strategy instruction that is structured, explicit, and systematic. Strategy instruction is critical for teaching all students a broader range of strategies than they use spontaneously, and for providing students with specific techniques for organization, planning, and self-checking.

Do Students Need Ongoing Strategy Instruction?

Every grade level heralds changes in the curriculum, the setting, the expectations, and in each student's developmental level. Students' learning profiles are not static, but often change as a function of the match or mismatch between the child's specific strengths and weaknesses and the demands of the classroom, the teacher, and the curriculum. Some students who exhibit no early school difficulties may suddenly flounder when the classroom demands change and require the coordination of many different subskills and strategies. In other words, learning disabilities may not become evident until the later grades, when changes in the setting and task demands stress a student's abilities to the extent that previously successful compensatory strategies are no longer effective.

Critical transition times in the curriculum—first grade, fourth grade, middle school, high school, and college—can be particularly problematic for students. Each of these transitions corresponds with increased organizational demands and the introduction of tasks that require the coordination and integration of multiple skills and strategies (e.g., complex writing assignments, book reports, and multiple-choice tests). Classroom teachers can help students to cope more effectively by modifying the classroom demands to accommodate students' rates and styles of learning.

....
Methods of Identifying Students' Learning Profiles

Effective teachers understand their students' strengths and weaknesses and adjust the classroom requirements to match their students' learning profiles. Some students exhibit learning profiles that are difficult to understand without assessment information elicited from formal tests or classroom-based assessment measures. Recently, performance-based assessment techniques and portfolio assessment methods (Wolf, LeMahieu, & Eresh, 1992) have become increasingly widespread as teachers develop greater proficiency in assessing their students informally as part of the daily curriculum.

Formal Assessment

Formal neuropsychological and educational testing often provides critical information about a student's learning style and helps teachers to understand why a particular student is struggling in the classroom. However, these assessments cannot provide all the answers. It is important to recognize that assessments are limited when they provide only scores and grade-level equivalents. Further, product-oriented tests do not clarify how the student is learning and why the student is experiencing difficulty. Assessments are most helpful when they are process oriented, focus on how the student learns, and provide specific educational recommendations that can be implemented in the classroom setting.

Teachers as Assessors

Effective teachers have always used informal assessment methods to gain an understanding of why and how a particular student may be struggling. The idea of "teachers as assessors" is becoming increasingly popular as Assessment for Teaching methods are developed (Meltzer, 1993a, 1993b; Roditi, 1993). Classroom-based assessment methods evaluate how students learn the required material and how effectively they retain and access knowledge.

Recognizing Students with Learning and Attentional Difficulties

No single academic profile characterizes all students with learning difficulties. Students with learning difficulties may have weaknesses in memory, language, auditory perception, and/or visual perception. Some are poor readers and spellers. Others have difficulty with written or oral expression. Still others cannot memorize math facts. Some students with learning difficulties may have weak organizational skills and may be erratic in their completion of homework assignments. Students with attentional weaknesses may have both academic and social difficulties. The one characteristic that all these students have in common is that, despite their average to above-average intellectual ability, they are delayed in reading, writing, mathematics, listening, and/or speaking skills. In other words, a

Table 1.1. How Learning Difficulties Manifest in the Classroom

Difficulties Students with LD Experience	How These Difficulties Affect Classroom Performance
• May process information in unique ways	• Inconsistent, discrepancies between in-class and test performance
• May process information at very slow rates	• Slow to volunteer, difficulty with timed tasks
• May have language-processing weaknesses	• May have difficulty following directions and may appear inattentive
• May have difficulties remembering rote information due to weaknesses in automatic memory	• Struggle to remember letter formations, math facts, days of week, months of the year
• May not develop efficient and effective strategies for completeing work	• Seem to lag behind others, slow to master strategies for learning; often masks their superior conceptual reasoning and problem solving
• May have difficulty shifting flexibly among different approaches	• Difficulty adjusting to new teachers and to new situations
• May not abandon strategies that are inefficient or ineffective	• May consistently solve problems the same way despite instruction in alternate strategies
• May struggle to prioritize and to focus on salient details	• May talk around issues, cannot summarize, poor study skills, poor outlining strategies, poor reading comprehension
• May be disorganized or may use different processing routes to organize information	• Book bags are messy, writing is disorganized, unprepared for classes
• May have difficulty coordinating the strategies needed to learn effectively	• Task performance inconsistent (e.g., 100% on spelling tests with single dictated words, but misspell these same words in the context of creative writing)
• Often unaware of the usefulness of specific planning and checking strategies	• Do not use prereading or prewriting strategies, do not edit
• May be impulsive and may not spontaneously plan their work	• Disorganized, difficulty budgeting their time
• May not spontaneously self-correct	• Carelessness with math, spelling, writing

Note. Specific classroom management strategies for students with LD are listed throughout this book. This list includes only selected difficulties that students experience.

Table 1.2. How Attentional Problems Manifest in the Classroom

Difficulties Students with Attention Problems Experience	How These Difficulties Affect Classroom Performance	Strategies to Assist Students with Attention Problems
Distractible	Daydream (distracted by inner thoughts) or attend to extraneous sounds or visual stimuli in the classroom	Make eye contact with students; check in with students frequently
Impulsive	Do not plan before beginning tasks May have social problems because of inappropriate comments May appear careless and inattentive to details	Preferential seating Teach planning and self-checking strategies (e.g., personalized checklists)
Disorganized	Lose work, forget homework, do not complete assignments	Teach organizational strategies (e.g., calendars, homework notebooks) Parents and teachers check homework regularly
Difficulty sustaining attention	Difficulty following through on long-term assignments Difficulty concentrating during classes with lecture formats May struggle to focus	Break down long-term projects into manageable steps Provide hands-on projects Cooperative learning Accompany oral presentations with visuals
May be fidgety and motorically active	Fidgety, move around, fiddle with objects	Provide legitimate opportunities to move around (e.g., chalkboard monitor or messenger)
Inconsistent performance	Work quality often inconsistent across tasks, settings, and situations May often repeat the same mistakes	Accept the variablity in students' performance

Note. (a) Many, but not all, of these students are diagnosed as ADD. (b) This list includes only a few selected strategies—see text for more detailed suggestions.

© 1996 PRO-ED, Inc.

significant discrepancy exists between ability and achievement. Most of these students have a combination of learning difficulties, the manifestation of which can vary enormously. Table 1.1 outlines the ways in which some students' learning difficulties may be exhibited in your classroom.

Many students with learning difficulties also experience attentional difficulties and may show excessive impulsivity, distractibility, and motor activity. These students may experience organizational difficulties, they may have problems staying on task, and they may have difficulties concentrating in group situations. These behavioral characteristics often lead to a diagnosis of attention deficit disorder (ADD). Most elusive and confusing to teachers are the students who show attentional problems but are not overactive. These students are often distractible, disorganized, or impulsive and show poor self-monitoring skills. They often overfocus on details so that they have difficulty identifying the global issues, and they become confused when too much information is presented. They are also extremely distractible and may appear to daydream so that instructions need to be repeated a number of times. As a result, tasks that require organization and prioritizing may be extremely difficult for them. Their academic problems are often attributed to low motivation, lack of effort, or lowered intellectual ability rather than to their attentional problems. Because they do not have behavior problems and their difficulties are often subtle, they may be ignored or misdiagnosed. Table 1.2 provides strategies for assisting students with ADD in the classroom.

Chapter 2

Techniques for Teaching Learning Strategies

As a teacher, you are the single most valuable resource your students have. This means that you will want to maximize the time you spend with your students, whether in small- or large-group instructional settings or in one-to-one situations. Most students with learning and attentional problems do not spontaneously organize their own work in response to the numerous demands of the classroom. This difficulty becomes increasingly problematic as students advance through the grades. When they reach middle school, they are required to meet the demands of many teachers who may have varying styles of instruction and different performance standards. Thus, the organization you provide is critically important in helping these students to become more effective learners.

Principles to Guide Strategy Instruction

Strategy instruction can be incorporated into the curriculum fairly readily when the curriculum content is used as a springboard for teaching students how to learn.

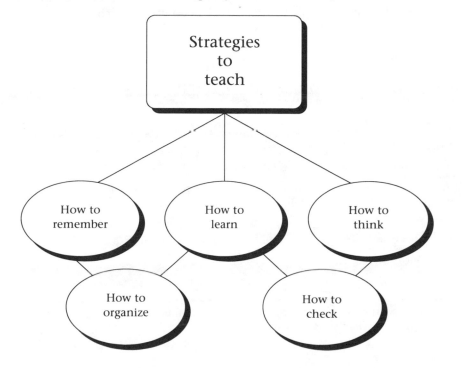

As you emphasize strategies in your classroom, you will find that content becomes less important than the processes and strategies students use to remember, think, problem-solve, organize, plan, self-check, and self-monitor. Effective learning strategies help all students learn how to learn and, furthermore, can be taught within the context of the daily curriculum. Students with learning and attentional problems often need more practice, repetition, and review than others when these strategies are taught in the classroom. Some of the principles underlying strategy instruction are listed in Table 2.1.

1. **Think big, start small.** Once you have adopted a "strategic" approach to accommodating the many different learning styles in your classroom, you will use this philosophy to make decisions about the way your class is structured. But, keep in mind that change occurs gradually, over time. Introduce a few new strategies that you feel are most critical to the needs of your students. Make a few modifications for students with learning difficulties who need them the most. When you feel comfortable with these, attempt a new strategy and add a few more modifications. Over time, you will develop a repertoire of strategies and modifications to use with the entire class or with individual students.

Table 2.1. Principles Underlying Strategy Instruction

- Encourage active learning (e.g., prereading, prewriting, cooperative learning groups).

- Review concepts and principles.

- Use a spiraled method of instruction (preface new material with review of previous work).

- Teach strategies in the context of the curriculum and not as a separate topic. For example, when students are required to complete independent research for a science project, teach strategies for highlighting, note taking, and organizing information.

- Teach strategies through modeling and direct explanations of procedures.

- Provide as much practice and review as possible so that students can apply the strategies they learn to a variety of different examples (e.g., strategies for active reading are practiced with science, social studies, history).

- Monitor students' practice in applying different strategies and provide helpful feedback.

- Teach preplanning and organizational strategies.

- Teach self-monitoring and self-checking strategies.

- Help students to experience mastery and success so that they understand the benefits of using specific strategies. This will insure that they value the strategy, use it consistently, and generalize the strategy to other tasks and settings.

- Communicate and collaborate with all involved professionals.

- Encourage continued use of and generalization of strategies.

- Emphasize the importance of automaticity in basic skills (math facts, spelling).

Note. Students with unique learning needs often need more repetition, greater intensity, and more structure when strategy instruction occurs.

2. **Individualizing does not mean making 20 to 30 individual lesson plans.** Absolutely *not!!* The idea behind strategic teaching is to make efficient use of *your* time as well as of your students' time and effort. Additionally, because strategies are best taught in context, strategic teaching involves integrating strategy instruction into your existing curriculum. This may require some modifications, rather than additions, to your present plans and materials. In other words, *you* can be strategic in the approach you take to everything including classroom seating and standardized testing.

3. **"Do what I say *and* do what I do."** One of the most effective and efficient ways to make your classroom a setting for strategic learning is to model strategic thinking processes for your students. Thinking aloud as you solve a problem offers your students a unique opportunity to witness problem-solving strategies in action. Too often students think teachers have all the answers, but they have no idea how teachers arrive at those answers! Your example can heighten students' awareness of their own metacognitive processes.

4. **Question your questions.** Think about your questioning techniques in the classroom. In addition to assessing students' knowledge of the content material, you can also engage your students in questions that will lead them to understand the processes involved in acquiring new information. For example, when a student gives a correct answer to your question on content, you can probe further by asking, "How did you arrive at that answer?" Your students will be encouraged to find that there are numerous ways to locate information in text. Alerting students to the processes involved in knowledge acquisition can lead them to be more efficient learners.

5. **Use positive approaches.** Explain expectations regarding behavior. Classroom rules should be stated in positive terms (i.e., *do*'s rather than *don't*'s), with positive and negative consequences explicitly expressed. Analyze students' performance within the context of their learning styles. Positive incentives may take longer to initiate and to achieve results, but they are more effective in the long run and help students to develop a sense of pride and responsibility. Further, if students are involved in setting goals and understand how specific strategies relate to their learning styles, they may be more motivated to change.

Teaching Organizational Strategies

As students advance into the fourth grade and beyond, an increasing emphasis is placed on long-term projects, independent work, book reports, and tasks that require planning, prioritizing, and organization. Many students begin to experience school problems for the first time and may show a range of organizational difficulties that often have a significant impact on their academic performance. You can help your students to develop more efficient work habits and to improve their organizational skills by incorporating a few simple techniques in the daily curriculum. These organizational strategies are important for all students and are particularly critical for students with learning and attentional difficulties.

Identifying Students with Organizational Difficulties

Students experience a wide range of organizational difficulties that affect their ability to plan, prioritize, and coordinate the many diverse requirements of the curriculum from the upper elementary grades onward. Some of these organizational difficulties are listed below.

Selected Organizational Difficulties That Affect Classroom Performance

❑ Students may have difficulty organizing and budgeting their time.

❑ Students may have trouble planning independently.

❑ Students may struggle to coordinate short-term and long-term assignments.

❑ Students may need help to insure that they continue to use organizational procedures in a sustained and systematic manner.

❑ Students may not record their homework assignments consistently.

❑ Students may write down only some of their homework assignments because of weaknesses in information processing and/or slow writing speed.

❑ Students may write down their homework assignments but forget their notebooks.

❑ Students may write down their homework assignments but forget the necessary books or papers at school.

❑ Students may complete their homework assignments but forget to hand these into the teacher.

❑ Students' desks, lockers, and book bags may be so messy and disorganized that they have trouble finding their belongings.

❑ Work may be often late or incomplete because of students' slow rate of processing.

❑ Students' work may seem messy; papers often may be crumpled or may show frequent erasures and cross-outs.

❑ The work students submit may not reflect their level of effort.

Improving the Organizational Strategies of Your Students

You can help your students improve their organizational skills by teaching them a few simple strategies that are often taken for granted. Remember that students with learning and attention problems often need more structure, repetition, and review than other students before they use these strategies independently. They also need frequent reminders to insure that they use the strategies you teach them for improving their organization. Selected organizational strategies are listed below.

Selected Organizational Strategies

❑ *Planning Calendars and Assignment Logs:* Teach students to record deadlines and due dates systematically.

❑ *Time Management:* Teach students to plan short- and long-term assignments.

❑ *Planning Long-Term Projects:* Teach students to budget their work time by providing phased time lines and study plans.

❑ *Budgeting Time:* Teach students to budget study time through consistent review, thereby preventing last-minute panic.

❑ *Homework Logs:* Teach students to record their homework assignments and a list of the books they need. They should also check off their logs after their work is completed and they have placed it in their school bags.

❑ *Test Preparation:* Teach short- and long-term planning strategies.

❑ *Organization:* Teach students a system for organizing their desks and lockers at school.

❑ *Notebooks and Folders:* Remember that different systems work for different students. For example, some students are successful with folders that are color-coded by subject, whereas others are systematic enough to utilize "Trapperkeepers."

❑ *Color-Coding:* Teach students to color-code materials for each class.

❑ *Checklists:* Teach students to tape checklists of items needed for each class to the front of the book used in that class.

The following organizational strategies may also be helpful:

- Encourage your students to try different organizers and organizational systems. Remember that individualized modifications may be needed for students with learning and attentional difficulties who may have difficulty with systems that work well for other students.

- Enforce the use of homework notebooks, which should be signed by parents and teachers on a daily basis. Students with learning difficulties require accountability and regular routines. These students often need outside reminders long after other students use these methods spontaneously. Remember that checking a student's homework notebook does not mean you are encouraging independence.

- Help your students to review or get started on their homework before they leave school. This will help them clarify their questions and confusions and approach their work in a more organized fashion.

- Help your students list their plans and priorities for multistep assignments. Modeling will help them schedule their work more easily and improve their time management.

- Teach students to develop their own personalized checklists for checking, correcting, and editing their work. Encourage them to paste these checklists into their notebooks.

- Teach your students strategies for note taking (two-column notes, mapping, webbing) and review these note-taking methods frequently. Remember that students with language-processing weaknesses often benefit from visual strategies such as maps and webs that summarize all critical information on a single page. However, students with weaknesses in visual processing become confused when visual arrays are used, and they benefit from systems that are more language-oriented (e.g., two-column notes). For these reasons, it is important to expose your students to a variety of methods and to allow each student to select a system that works for him or her.

- Teach your students outlining techniques because these enforce structure, highlight major themes, and provide categories for organizing information. Remember that students with learning and attentional problems need more review and practice with these techniques.

Steps to Strategic Classroom Organization

1. **Implement preferential seating when necessary.** Be aware of each student's level of involvement during different tasks. Are your students all actively engaged in the lesson, or is the dialogue primarily confined to a core set of students? During independent work periods, are students completing the

assignment accurately and efficiently? Some students may benefit from preferential seating to accommodate their learning styles. For example, students with language-processing difficulties may need to be closer to the teacher, where they can pick up visual cues and receive redirection when necessary. Students with attentional weaknesses may need to be seated away from noisy or distracting areas of the classroom. In fact, you may want to group students' desks according to their preferred learning styles. Establish eye contact with students and circulate around the room.

2. **Use flexible groupings for strategy instruction.** Placing students in smaller groups for instruction is a common instructional practice. Often, the criteria for these groups has been ability level (e.g., *low, middle, high*). With flexible groupings, groups can be formed and disbanded for a variety of purposes. Students can be grouped together to learn a specific skill or strategy. Another set of groups can be formed according to the strategies students prefer to use for a given task. Or, you may teach two strategies for the same task and then divide the class into groups. Each group could try a different strategy. Students could then report on the benefits and drawbacks of that strategy to the larger group. As different students report their reasons for preferring one strategy over another, they are also giving you information about their learning styles.

3. **Use strategy practice labs.** Practice labs offer a chance for students to apply the different strategies you have taught them. With practice, many strategies can become automatic, and students will also begin to see the efficacy of certain strategies for use in certain tasks. For example, designate one class period per week as strategy lab time. Allow the students to experiment with a learning strategy that is useful for your content material.

4. **Capitalize on seatwork opportunities.** It is important that students learn to apply strategies independently and with confidence. Purposeful, well-directed seatwork can be a vehicle for strategy instruction. In addition to allowing you to check students' recall of information, seatwork can also include instruction in the use of strategies. This allows you time to work with other students, while still providing practice in critical thinking skills for independent work.

5. **Use checklists and contracts.** Checklists help students assume additional responsibility for their academic progress and behavior. Create checklists with your students that target a few key goals. State expectations in positive terms (e.g., "Will turn in rough draft of assignment on Friday" instead of "Will not turn in late assignments"; or "Will check capitalization on each paper" instead of "Will not make punctuation errors"). Design the checklist for success by setting reasonable goals that you and your students agree are attainable. Feel free to add to the checklists as the students master the initial goals. Permit your students to earn rewards, such as free time or computer time, for their progress.

Contracts are similar to checklists and offer another way to assist your students in becoming more self-directed. Once you and your student have decided on the terms for a contract, student and teacher responsibilities are outlined in writing. Both sign the agreement, which is designed to be reviewed at certain times. As with the checklists, rewards are specified. Each of these systems allows students to develop responsibility and control over their academic progress and behavior.

6. **Make classroom assignments strategic.** You don't have to make dramatic changes in your assignments. Simple modifications can dramatically enhance the strategic instruction in your classroom. Examples of modifications are as follows:

   - Select the workbook pages that are best suited to develop strategy use by your students, rather than assigning all of the pages of the workbook.

   - Modify worksheet instructions to emphasize strategic thinking. In this way, you can keep the same materials, but alter the focus of the lesson from straight recall to process thinking (i.e., from testing to teaching).

   - Consider assigning fewer math problems or English exercises. The additional time this allows can be redirected to the practice of strategies in that specific content area.

   - Provide a systematic and consistent structure for giving and recording classroom assignments. Use multiple methods to assign homework. Explain the assignment. Write it on the board. Insist that students write it down. If possible, insist they maintain some form of an assignment notebook. Check to see that assignments have been recorded before students leave your class.

7. **Make accommodations for individual learning needs.** Students who have difficulty with their rate of work or the motor demands of writing may need to have their workload reduced. For example, these students may be expected to complete only the even-numbered problems or the critical questions. Involve the students in the process of making these modifications and clearly articulate your expectations to students.

   Students with reading difficulties may need more significant modifications. For example, students with good conceptualization abilities but severe decoding weaknesses may benefit from listening to their textbooks on tape (available from Recordings for the Blind). Alternate texts with similar themes can be assigned. Students can maintain learning logs rather than answering specific questions; alternately, peers could read the questions to them. (See the Recommended Reading section at the end of the manual for additional suggestions.)

8. **Collaborate with the members of your team.** Communication among teachers is a major key to success for many students with learning difficulties. Find out what your colleagues are expecting from the students. Whenever possible, coordinate your demands with those of other teachers. Try not to schedule major due dates within the same week. Find out how your students are doing in other classes. You may find that a student who struggles in your class is successful in another class. There may be elements of another teacher's style that you can incorporate for use with a particular student. Alternatively, you may offer insights about successes you have had with a student that can assist another teacher who is struggling with the same student. Organize regular meetings to insure that you all use a team approach for addressing the needs of your students with learning problems.

9. **Communicate regularly with parents.** Parents often struggle at home when helping their children complete homework and study for tests. Offer guidelines to parents at the beginning of the year about your expectations regarding their involvement. How much help should parents give? How much time should homework be expected to take? Offer suggestions as to how parents can set up an optimal homework environment at home (e.g., a study space free of distractions, a routine for homework completion).

   Teach students study strategies and inform parents about the ways in which they can help students apply these strategies at home (e.g., with a question-and-answer format, parents can ask their children the questions). Encourage parents to contact you if students are having problems with homework demands, and make modifications as appropriate.

   Inform parents when students have improved in their strategy use. Too often, parents hear from teachers only when difficulties arise. Informing parents of positive achievements will encourage them to remain involved and enhance the student's self-esteem.

   Inform parents in the early stages when problems in learning and behavior come up. When a problem develops, it is always best to "nip it in the bud" before it becomes too difficult to remediate. Contacting the parent may provide insight into the nature of the problem and assist you in developing effective solutions. This also indicates to the student that all adults are working together as a team.

   For some students, a communication notebook may be necessary. Teachers, parents, and older students could agree about the frequency of communication (e.g., every day, once a week) and record pertinent information, accentuating any positive improvements.

10. **Focus on the process.** Allow projects to be completed in a process fashion. In other words, break long-term assignments into smaller units and set goals and deadlines for each phase. Develop study plans with students to help them accomplish each goal. Collect and assess students' work throughout the project, rather than solely at completion. This will allow you to gauge students'

understanding of the assignment and their progress toward completion. You will also learn quickly which students need additional direction or lack specific skills needed to complete sections of an assignment. This can save you precious time grading the final outcome. This can also alleviate the frustration of many students with learning disabilities. These students may work diligently, but without the understanding or strategies they need. Therefore, they are prone to fail an evaluation that considers only the final product. At other times, you may want to allow students to have the option of submitting work at draft stages or simply turning in a completed assignment.

11. **Allow some freedom of choice.** Remember that no one strategy works for everyone. Allowing students to make choices engages them in the learning process and encourages them to consider their thinking and learning in a new and hopefully more purposeful manner.

12. **Be direct. Be strategic. Keep it simple.** Keep in mind the importance of being direct with your students about the *how* of learning, in addition to the what of learning. If you and your students are to be successful with strategy instruction, it is also important to keep the task simple. Teach only a few strategies at a time and allow many opportunities for practice and generalization of strategies before moving on to others.

Empowering Students to Become Independent Learners and Self-Advocates

The success of strategy instruction is usually influenced by students' ability to generalize strategies and to value and "own" the strategies they are taught. Self-awareness is therefore a critical component of successful strategy instruction, which depends heavily on students' willingness to make the necessary effort to apply a specific strategy consistently. Self-awareness and recognition of the value of using specific strategies are also extremely important because of the initial increase in work time that is involved as students learn new routines. For example, when students begin to use a planning strategy to organize their written output (e.g., drawing maps and webs), there is an initial increase in work time. Speed and efficiency are sacrificed to insure greater accuracy. However, use of a systematic method insures that students become increasingly efficient over time, which eventually decreases their work time. One of the most difficult challenges of strategy instruction, therefore, is to help students to develop patience and to delay gratification. Fairly rapid success as a result of using a strategy usually helps students to value specific strategies and to expend the necessary effort to use these strategies.

In order to help your students to become independent learners and self-advocates, it is important to understand their perceptions of their own abilities and their views of the strategies that they use to accomplish different academic tasks. Do they have realistic judgments of the important components of classroom learning? Do they recognize the importance of using specific strategies? Do they use different strategies for completing various academic tasks? For example, studies have shown that some students consider a good reader as someone who reads quickly and a good writer as somebody with neat handwriting. Some students recognize the importance of using specific learning strategies, whereas other students do not implement any strategies as they complete different academic tasks.

How Students View Their Own Abilities

Students can become independent learners only when they understand their learning profiles, maintain positive views of their own competence, and are aware of the unique demands of different learning situations. Self-awareness is a critical precursor to the strategies that underlie effective learning—namely, planning, monitoring, checking, and evaluating outcomes. Students' use of particular strategies also is associated with their feelings of empowerment in the learning situation and their willingness to invest the effort needed to use the strategies that are important for success.

Self-esteem and motivation also affect the learning process in very important ways and often interact with students' willingness to use strategies in their classrooms. Successful learners frequently attribute their successes to effort and their failures to lack of effort, and are therefore more likely to use strategies actively. In contrast, students with learning difficulties often experience consistent failure over the years, which negatively affects their self-perceptions and self-esteem. Some students believe they are "dumb" and attribute their failure to insufficient ability rather than limited effort or different learning styles (Licht, 1993). As a result of this "learned helplessness," they may become anxious and fearful of failure, with the result that they are unlikely to use active problem-solving strategies and likely to avoid challenging tasks (Licht, 1993).

How can teachers and professionals access students' perceptions?

The Strategy Observation System

The *Strategy Observation System* (SOS; Meltzer, 1993c, in press; Meltzer & Roditi, in press) is a series of questionnaires designed by the staff at ResearchILD to identify students' and teachers' perceptions of strategic learning. The SOS includes three questionnaires: (a) the Student Self-Report System (SSRS), (b) the Teacher Observation System (TOS), and (c) the Survey of Strategy Awareness (SOSA). This set of questionnaires assesses teachers' judgments of students' strategy use as well as students' self-perceptions of their strategy use.

The Student Self-Report System (SSRS).   The SSRS samples students' views of their learning strategies and work habits in reading, writing, spelling, math, and general organization. The SSRS has been pilot tested over the past 2 years and is currently being used in a large study as part of the *Strategies for Success* program (Meltzer et al., 1994). This system can help you understand your students' judgments of their ability and strategies in reading, writing, spelling, study skills, and organization. Examples of items from the SSRS are shown below.

Sample Items from the SSRS

❑ After I read, I try to tell the story in my own words.

❑ When I read, I ask myself questions to help me remember.

❑ Before I begin to read my textbook, I look at the headings and pictures to get an idea about what I will be reading.

❑ When I have to write a paper for school, I don't know where to begin.

❑ Before I write, I plan my ideas on paper.

❑ When I am writing, I forget how to spell words.

❑ I use tricks to help me remember math facts.

❑ I have a step-by-step plan before I start solving a math word problem.

❑ I check my work before turning it in.

❑ I make a plan before I begin my homework.

© 1996 PRO-ED, Inc.

The Teacher Observation System (TOS).   The second questionnaire developed at ResearchILD as part of the SOS is the TOS, which provides teachers with a method of rating students' strategy use systematically. The TOS helps teachers observe and analyze students' efficiency and flexibility in strategic learning as well as their self-monitoring strategies. Teachers observe students' learning strategies and work habits in reading, writing, spelling, math, and general organization. The TOS is closely linked to the SSRS so that comparisons between teacher and student perceptions can be made. The following are sample items from the TOS.

Sample Items from the TOS

❏ Readily completes reading assignments.

❏ Uses outlines to organize writing.

❏ Completed work has been proofread for spelling and punctuation.

❏ Corrects spelling errors systematically.

❏ Uses strategies (e.g., pictures) to solve word problems.

❏ Comes to class prepared.

Both the SSRS and the TOS are currently being pilot tested in a number of Massachusetts school systems. To date, teacher comments have indicated that these surveys provide information that is extremely helpful for understanding the strategies students use in the learning situation. Inventories like this can help teachers understand and address the diverse needs of students in their classrooms.

The Survey of Strategy Awareness (SOSA). The SOSA has been designed to identify teachers' knowledge and understanding of strategy use before and after the implementation of the *Strategies for Success* program. The SOSA identifies teachers' understanding and philosophy about the importance of teaching learning strategies in the classroom as well as the extent to which they teach particular strategies.

By understanding how students view themselves as learners and what strategies they believe they use, teachers can help students become more strategic in the classroom. The following list is a summary of a few of the major principles for helping students with learning difficulties become more strategic in the classroom setting.

How to Help Students with LD
Become Strategic Learners

❑ Help students understand their profiles of strengths and weaknesses in the learning situation. They need help in recognizing that their learning difficulties bear no relationship to their intelligence, and that their strong intellectual ability will help them to overcome their processing and strategic weaknesses.

❑ Help students recognize and accept that their learning styles are different from those of other students. They need to use alternate strategies and may need classroom accommodations that match their learning styles. Students must also accept the fact that these classroom accommodations may single them out as different and may sometimes draw attention to their learning styles.

❑ Help empower students to become self-advocates so that they will request the necessary accommodations in all their classes.

❑ Insure that students experience success; this will help them believe in the value of their efforts and recognize that their efforts will lead to success.

❑ Encourage students to recognize that if they are slow to complete certain tasks, they may need to ask all their teachers for more time on tests at the high elementary, middle, and high school levels. If oral examinations are also helpful for them, students could be encouraged to discuss their learning difficulties with their teachers so that appropriate accommodations can be implemented. When these students are provided with the necessary support and encouragement, they will feel more comfortable about being singled out from their peers, which is an extremely sensitive issue at these higher age levels.

❑ Encourage students to request preferential seating if they experience difficulty getting attention in a group setting.

❑ Encourage students to move to a quiet part of the classroom if necessary.

(continued)

❏ Encourage students to discuss their homework assignments at appropriate times with you or with their classmates.

❏ Help students recognize the importance of self-correcting and self-checking and help them implement appropriate strategies.

❏ Help students develop personalized checklists to correct their work.

❏ Encourage students to understand the importance of taking risks in different learning situations.

❏ Help students understand the importance of strategic learning.

❏ Help students recognize the importance of shifting strategies and approaches based on the situational and task demands.

❏ Help students believe in themselves and recognize themselves as active learners.

Section II

Selected Learning Strategies

Chapter 3

Decoding and Spelling Strategies

Why teach strategies in decoding and spelling? Recently, there has been increasing evidence that phonological awareness (i.e., the awareness of distinct sounds within words and the ability to manipulate these sounds) is significantly correlated with early reading success. In fact, phonological awareness may be one of the best predictors of early reading success (Stanovich, 1986). Children demonstrate phonological awareness through activities such as rhyming, segmenting words or word groups into smaller parts, and generating words from a given sound. Children who can analyze component sounds in words and "play with" these sounds are often successful when they learn to read (Wolf & Dickinson, 1985).

Students with learning difficulties often show weaknesses in auditory processing abilities, which contribute to their difficulties with phonological awareness. They may have problems segmenting words and blending sounds into words. They may also have difficulties with auditory memory, discrimination, and sequencing. These weaknesses make it difficult for these students to access the speech sounds that make up words and to learn the corresponding letter patterns that represent these sounds. Consequently, they have difficulty acquiring early reading and spelling skills.

Attempts to circumvent these difficulties by teaching students through their stronger modalities (e.g., visual "sight word" approaches) have achieved less than satisfactory results. To become independent readers, students must at some point learn that the spelling patterns they see in print map onto sounds they hear in speech. This understanding may be accomplished directly through instruction or indirectly through deduction. Students with strong skills in phonological awareness appear to acquire early reading skills because they are able to infer sound–symbol relationships, regardless of the reading methods used. Similarly, students may be strong in spelling because they can use their knowledge of sound–symbol correspondence rules to write words.

Students with learning difficulties may not readily make these inferences. They may have difficulty segmenting words into their component sounds, remembering sound–symbol correspondence rules, and generalizing the variations in phoneme productions (e.g., the short /a/ in *bat* is different from the short /a/ in *ban*). This results in reading and spelling difficulties. Spelling skills may also be affected by weak visual memory, which makes it difficult for students to remember the visual representations of words and to reproduce these when spelling.

Despite these difficulties, it is critical that students with learning disabilities (LD) learn to decode and to spell so that they can become independent, fluent readers and writers. Students with and without learning difficulties progress through similar stages during the development of reading and spelling skills (Chall, 1983), so it is important for students with learning difficulties to master the alphabetic principles that make up words. However, they may need more explicit instruction than their peers.

How do you teach decoding and spelling? Although many reading programs teach decoding, not all of these programs use a systematic procedure. Furthermore, reading and spelling are often taught as separate subjects, and connections are rarely drawn between them. However, if spelling skills are taught in conjunction with decoding skills, students may more readily apply these skills during independent reading and writing tasks.

••

Examining Your Current Reading and Spelling Program

1. **Determine the type of reading program you teach.**

    - Does it teach decoding in a systematic way, or does it rely on students to infer these rules through whole-word or whole-text methods?

    - Does it provide enough structure for some of your students?

    - Can additional structure be provided for those who need it?

    For phonics programs:

    - Does this provide a systematic, structured, and stepwise introduction to the basic phonic rules?

    - What is the sequence of skills taught?

    - Are the skills taught relevant, or is there "overkill" in the scope and sequence (e.g., emphasizes low-frequency letter patterns)?

    - Is this a multisensory program?

    - Does the program use mnemonics (memory aids) or "key words" to help students remember sound–symbol correspondences?

    - Are there sufficient opportunities for oral reading in context in order to develop fluency?

    For whole-word or whole-language programs:

    - Can modifications be made to teach decoding skills directly to those who need it?

- Is decoding utilized as a strategy for discerning unknown words?

- Is the use of context clues recommended as a strategy for discerning unknown words above all other strategies? (Students with learning difficulties often over-rely on context to compensate for their difficulties with decoding. This may result in less efficient reading over time.)

- Are sufficient opportunities present for oral reading in context to develop fluency?

2. **Determine the type of spelling program you teach.**

   - Does this program use word lists that are grouped by a common rule or theme?

   - Do the rules parallel those taught in the reading program?

   - Are the words meaningful to students? Do they represent words that students need to learn how to spell?

   - Are there opportunities to individualize word lists?

   - Is there a pretest component, as well as meaningful activities for students who don't need to study all of the words?

   - Can students read all of the words they are expected to spell?

3. **Determine which rules need to be emphasized.**

   - Can the rules that are taught be generalized to a large number of words? Some students with learning difficulties may need more emphasis on spelling patterns that can be generalized easily (e.g., vowel combinations and syllabication skills) and less emphasis on patterns that are difficult to apply (e.g., making the schwa sound or writing accent marks). Keep in mind the purpose of the program should be to teach students the skills they need to decode and spell new words. An overemphasis on phonics with little emphasis on other components of reading and spelling can confuse and overload students.

   - Are opportunities present for students to use inductive reasoning to analyze rules? Students may remember a rule better if they are able to figure out the rule themselves when given a list of words.

4. **Use writing activities and invented spellings.** Students who frequently engage in writing are required to focus on sound–symbol relationships for meaningful purposes. They should be encouraged to use invented spellings when necessary, as this directs their attention to the phonological level of words.

Examining the Strengths and Weaknesses of Students

1. **Use a structured, multisensory program with students who have severe deficits in phonological awareness.** A specialized program such as Orton-Gillingham (Orton, 1966), Project Read (Green & Enfield, 1986), Wilson (Wilson, 1988), or Auditory Discrimination in Depth (Lindamood & Lindamood, 1975) may be necessary for some students to acquire decoding skills. Often, programs like these are provided by a learning disabilities specialist who has been appropriately trained. The regular classroom teacher and learning disabilities specialist can work together to develop a comprehensive program that provides a variety of activities for the student with learning difficulties to learn decoding skills and comprehension strategies. Each teacher can support the development of these skills and strategies in either setting.

   In many classrooms, interest in structured phonics has extended to the regular classroom setting. For example, Project Read has been designed for use in the regular classroom and is based on principles from the Orton-Gillingham program.

2. **Use language-rich texts for students with language difficulties.**

   - Supplement the structured phonics program with student-authored texts through a modified language experience approach. Students can write or dictate their own stories, which can then be compiled into a book for rereading. Words from these stories that share phonic principles with those words taught in the structured program can be integrated into phonics and spelling lessons.

   - Use trade books classified as early readers for independent reading.

   - Read frequently to students so that they hear the vocabulary, syntax, and text structure of literature (see below).

3. **Bypass decoding difficulties to enhance comprehension strategies.** Students whose decoding abilities lag behind their comprehension abilities also need to participate regularly in listening activities that introduce them to the language of literacy.

   - Teachers could read interesting literature to students to familiarize them with the vocabulary, syntax, and text structures of various genres.

   - Active comprehension strategies outlined in the next section can be taught through listening activities so that the students' interest in reading and development of active strategies continues to grow.

Modifying Your Program to Accommodate Individual Needs

1. **Help students develop "spelling consciousness" by teaching the basic rules for decoding and spelling.** For all grades, determine which students would benefit from direct instruction in decoding and spelling rules. In Grades 1 through 3, this instruction could be part of the core curriculum. Beyond Grade 3, analysis of students' errors on oral reading and spelling tasks will indicate which students may need systematic instruction.

   - Teach consonant patterns: initial and final position, consonant blends, digraphs, and irregular forms (e.g., silent letters, two sounds of *c/g*, etc.).

   - Teach vowel patterns: short, long, digraphs, diphthongs, r-controlled.

   - Teach the rules for adding suffixes and inflectional endings to root words with the following characteristics:

     —Drop the *e* in words with "silent e" (e.g., *shining*).

     —Change the *y* to *i* in words that end in a *y* preceded by a consonant (e.g., *dries*).

     —Double the final consonant in words with short vowels (e.g., *running*).

     —Form plurals with *es* for words ending in *x, s, sh, ch* (e.g., *foxes*); for words ending in *f*, change to *v* and add *es* (e.g., *gloves*).

   - Teach capitalization and punctuation rules that have implications for spelling (e.g., capitalization of proper nouns, use of the apostrophe, periods in abbreviations).

   - Develop mnemonics or key words for sound–symbol correspondences. Vowel patterns are often difficult for students with LD to remember. Students may benefit from multisensory strategies to remember these. Be sure that key words for vowels represent true sounds of the vowel (e.g., short /i/ is better represented in words like *it* and *Indian* than *igloo* and *ink*).

     Students also may benefit from the use of mnemonics or catchy phrases (e.g., "The principal is your pal"); homonyms (e.g., *heard–ear, herd–shepherd*); or rules of thumb (*i* before *e* except after *c* or when sounding like *a* as in *neighbor* and *weigh*). Mnemonic aids are often most effective when developed by the student.

2. **Develop syllabication principles.**

   - Focus on the efficient use of syllabication as a decoding and spelling strategy. It is important for students to understand the principles of syllabication and to be able to break longer words into component parts. The accuracy of correct syllabication may be less important. Keep in mind that the objective is to create more manageable units for decoding and spelling.

- Teach students to look for derivations of words. Recognizing compound words can facilitate the decoding and spelling of these words. For multisyllabic words containing roots and prefixes or suffixes, students can be taught to look for the roots and the affixes during reading and spelling. This may help them break words into meaningful units for reading and spelling (e.g., *know–known*). This is particularly helpful for identifying reduced vowels in unaccented syllables (e.g., *compete–competition*), silent letters (e.g., *govern–government*), and less typical patterns (e.g., *music–musician*). Through activities such as these, the schwa sound or accenting need not be taught as a rule, but the concept is developed through practical application.

3. **Develop fluency and accuracy for reading and spelling words in connected text.**

   - *Collaborative oral reading:* Students take turns reading with a teacher or peer who can model appropriate rate, phrasing, and intonation. Choose easier materials to develop fluency and more challenging materials to develop accuracy.

   - *Assisted reading:* Students read difficult text with a teacher or peer who maintains fluency by supplying words when students falter. This is particularly helpful for students who are mainstreamed for content area subjects but have difficulty reading the texts.

   - *Repeated readings:* The teacher reads a passage while students follow along. Then students read the passage on their own.

   - *Dictation:* Sentences can be individualized by using a student or tape recorder to dictate sentences.

   - *In-context spelling:* The teacher models the strategies he or she uses for spelling difficult words, incorporating skills taught for words in isolation. Students also share their strategies. The use of modeling helps students develop self-monitoring and helps them apply strategies in a flexible manner.

4. **Develop fluency and accuracy for reading and spelling words in isolation.**

   - Use words from content-area subjects, word banks, and frequently misspelled words for timed word recognition drills.

   - Teach students to use analogy when reading or spelling unfamiliar words. For example, students can identify words that rhyme with the target word and use these to figure out the new word (i.e., the "rhyming strategy").

• Create individualized spelling lists. Pair students to pre- and post-test each other on individual words.

• Teach visualization strategies for learning the spellings of new words. Students repeat the letter sequence aloud while looking at the word, then close their eyes and repeat the letter sequence again several times while mentally picturing the word. They could then write the word and compare this spelling with the model.

• Keep a notebook of frequently misspelled words. Students maintain this personalized spell-checker and refer to it when writing. Words commonly misspelled by the class can be posted in the room.

5. Teach students to self-monitor and alternate strategies when needed.

• Develop self-monitoring abilities.

—*Decoding:* Encourage students to check that their responses are real words and that they fit the contexts of the reading ("Does it make sense?").

—*Spelling:* When editing for spelling, students could circle all words they believe are spelled incorrectly and attempt to correct these or use a hand-held electronic spell-checker or a dictionary. Students who make frequent reversals can be taught strategies to help them remember the spatial orientation of these letters. For example, the "bed" strategy is effective for remembering *b/d*. These can be developed with the student. A second grader who frequently confused *h* and *n* developed the strategy "*h* has a handle" with the assistance of his teacher.

• Apply decoding/spelling rules in a flexible manner.

—*Decoding:* When decoding multisyllabic words with VCV patterns, both short and long sounds can be tried (e.g., "Decide before you divide: ca-mel? or cam-el?"). (This is also appropriate for hard/soft sounds of *c* and *g*.) When accenting words, students can be encouraged to try variations until a real word is found.

—*Spelling:* Students could try out the different spellings of a word until they found one that they believe is correct (i.e., the "have-a-go" strategy).

Chapter 4

Strategies for Improving Reading Comprehension

In this chapter we discuss the important components of reading comprehension. Reading involves many complex processes. We will examine these processes and discuss effective strategies for teaching reading comprehension.

What Are the Important Components of Reading Comprehension?

- ❑ Establishing purpose
- ❑ Relating text to prior experience
- ❑ Looking for author's viewpoint
- ❑ Extracting main ideas from text
- ❑ Disregarding less relevant details
- ❑ Ordering details hierarchically
- ❑ Prioritizing
- ❑ Evaluating
- ❑ Analyzing how effects are achieved

How Can You Help Students Develop Effective Reading Strategies?

- ❑ Evaluate your materials.
- ❑ Teach prereading strategies (e.g., set purposes for reading, preview vocabulary, activate prior knowledge).
- ❑ Teach active reading strategies (e.g., self-questioning, backtracking, margin notes, skim, rap and map, imagery).
- ❑ Discuss critical vocabulary before reading.
- ❑ Teach postreading strategies (e.g., question-answering, summarization, imagery).
- ❑ Teach specific strategies for analyzing narrative texts (e.g., fiction) and expository texts.

Why Teach Strategies in Reading Comprehension?

Historically, reading comprehension instruction has emphasized the importance of responding to questions at the end of text. Papers were graded and returned with little attention to how students arrived at their answers. Yet, reading involves complex processes and requires the use of many strategies.

Recently, teachers have begun to redefine their reading goals to include higher level thinking and critical reading. Students are expected not only to recognize words and understand what they read, but also to critique and evaluate reading material and to develop student-centered purposes for reading. To accomplish these goals, students must be able to regulate their own reading processes and to take control of their own involvement in this process. In other words, students must know *what* strategies to use as well as *how* and *when* to use them. This is called self-regulation.

Reading is complex and involves the integration of many thought processes. Various processes are emphasized throughout reading:

Before Reading

❏ Establishing purpose

❏ Relating to prior experience

❏ Looking for author's point of view

During Reading

❏ Extracting main ideas from text

❏ Disregarding less relevant details

❏ Ordering details hierarchically

❏ Prioritizing

After Reading

❏ Evaluating

❏ Studying parts in relation to whole

❏ Analyzing how effects are achieved

❏ Applying independent judgments

(adapted from Squire, 1984)

Yet, there is good news! Strategy instruction has been shown to be effective for improving reading ability for all students and especially for students with reading and learning problems (see Pressley & Harris, 1990).

How can assessment improve strategy instruction? Students with learning difficulties often have had individual psycho-educational assessments that can assist your understanding of how they learn best. Most of your students will have had only standardized group testing. This information can help you understand each of your students' strengths and weaknesses, and can often confirm what you have observed informally. Although grade equivalents provide little information in and of themselves, you can get a sense of individual student profiles by contrasting student performance on the different components of reading.

- Is there a discrepancy between the student's word identification skills and comprehension?

- Does the student have a good understanding of word meanings but not of connected text?

- Can the student answer literal questions, whereas making inferences is difficult for him or her?

Formal reading assessment cannot, however, inform you as to which strategies a student is using effectively and how active he or she is in the process. So how can you find this out? You can measure this informally by analyzing each student's performance and error patterns during the reading process.

Does the student:

- read fluently and automatically so that attention can be focused on meaning (decode text)?

- self-correct oral reading errors?

- ask questions when confused?

- return to the text to clarify information?

- summarize accurately?

Information gained through formal and informal assessment can be used to help you plan instruction that capitalizes on students' strengths and develops weaker areas. Knowing which strategies students use effectively and which strategies they lack will help you develop lessons that enable all students to become active, strategic readers (see Table 4.1).

Table 4.1. A Comparison of Skilled Readers with Students
Who Have Difficulties

Skilled readers . . .	Students with reading difficulties . . .
• move in and out of many reading processes in a recursive manner.	• may become overwhelmed by the many processes interacting during reading.
• know how and when to use specific strategies.	• may have difficulty alternating strategies due to limited flexibility.
• identify which strategies are needed for a particular reading selection.	• may have difficulty selecting appropriate reading strategies at different times.
• monitor and evaluate their use of strategies constantly.	• may not use strategies to help them become actively involved.
• relate new information to what is known throughout the reading process.	• may have limited background knowledge or may have difficulty accessing what they know.
• make predictions and confirm these predictions while reading	• may not recognize when they have collected sufficient information to form a hypothesis.
• ask themselves questions and recognize main themes.	• may overfocus on details and miss main themes.
• sort through and integrate the many clues provided in the text.	• may have difficulty prioritizing information and sorting through multiple details.
• monitor their level of understanding (e.g., "know when they don't know").	• may struggle to integrate all the information and to monitor their own understanding at the same time.
• make evaluations and judgments about what is read.	• may lack the confidence to develop their own thoughts and opinions.

How Can You Help Your Students Develop Effective Reading Strategies?

A. Evaluate your curriculum.

B. Teach prereading strategies.

C. Teach active reading strategies.

D. Teach postreading strategies.

E. Expand vocabulary knowledge.

A. Evaluation of Your Curriculum

The following procedures will help you evaluate your curriculum:

1. Determine whether the reading level of selected material is appropriate.

- Listen to individual students read orally and note errors. If the student mispronounces more than 10% of the words, the text is too difficult.

- Determine readability using the Fry Readability formula (see Appendix 1).

- Check comprehension ability. Students should be able to answer literal and inferential questions with at least 70% accuracy.

If the text is too difficult for some students, think of ways to make it accessible to these students. Can you do any of the following?

- Develop study guides.

- Teach key vocabulary and concepts.

- Use peer tutoring.

- Put the selection on tape.

- Find alternate texts.

- Supplement the text with audiovisual aids.

- Copy and enlarge pages of text to help students keep their places and write notes.

2. **Use materials that are well structured and have appropriate, understandable language.**

- Are the ideas expressed explicitly?

- Can you recognize the text structure?

- If fiction, does the material follow a predictable story sequence or is it episodic?

- If nonfiction, is it organized chronologically, cause–effect, or comparison/contrast?

3. **Begin strategy instruction with small segments of text.** Decide which strategies students will need in order to comprehend the material.

- Does the material require a lot of background knowledge?

- Does it contain content-specific vocabulary?

- Is there heavy emphasis on figurative language?

- Are there many facts to remember?

4. **Decide which students will need specific instruction in these strategies.**

••

B. Prereading Strategies

Prereading strategies can include the following:

Prereading Strategies

❏ Set purposes for reading.

❏ Preview vocabulary.

❏ Activate prior knowledge.

❏ Link known knowledge to new knowledge.

---

1. **Set Purposes for Reading—Grades 1–12.** Students with LD often begin reading without determining *why* they are reading or *what* they expect to find out. This negatively affects how much they remember and understand.

Preview Text: Read titles, read headings and subheadings, look at pictures, skim introductions and conclusions, read questions embedded in the text or located at the end of the chapter.

Make Predictions: Use previewing to form hypotheses and create questions about the reading. Set learning goals: "What do I want to learn?" "What do I expect to find out?"

2. Preview Vocabulary—Grades 1–12

Vocabulary Splash: List key words from the selection. Students discuss the word meanings and synonyms. Students record these words and meanings on index cards to develop a word bank. They create novel sentences or paragraphs containing the words. This is particularly helpful for students with LD who need to develop a broader vocabulary base.

At the secondary level, students can predict words that will be used in the selection based on chapter titles and headings. Students who are reluctant to contribute can be led through word associations by being asked, "What does [content-specific word] remind you of?" After reading, students note which words were actually found in the selection (Kaplan & Tuchman, 1985).

3. Activate Prior Knowledge—Grades 1–12

Brainstorming: Provide key concepts from the passage to be read, and ask students to think of as many words as they can that are related to the stimulus word (see Figure 4.1). These can be written by each student before a group discussion or recorded as a group. Students can share their word lists with the group and write paragraphs using the words. By writing the words first, students with LD who are slower to process and respond can contribute equally.

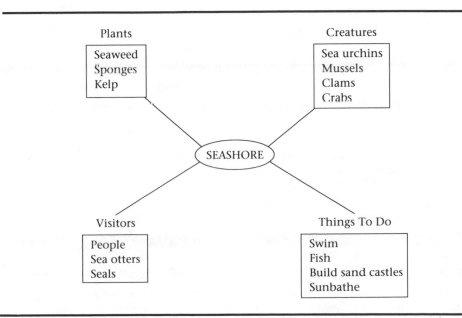

Figure 4.1. Before the lesson, students brainstorm knowledge.

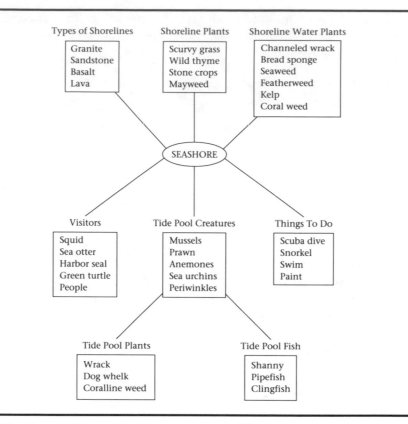

Figure 4.2. After the lesson, new concepts are added.

4. Link Known Knowledge to New Knowledge—Grades 1–12

Semantic Mapping: As students share their words from the brainstorming activity, words are grouped in categories as a master map is made. The teacher can, at any time, add his or her words to the map. The interrelationships among the words are discussed, including similarities and differences. Attention is then focused on those categories that are most relevant to the themes in reading (see Figure 4.2). This is particularly helpful for students with learning difficulties who need to develop depth of vocabulary knowledge (Johnson, n.d.).

C. Active Reading Strategies

1. **Self-Questioning—Grades 1–12.** Skilled readers engage in self-regulation throughout the reading process by monitoring their own level of understanding and taking corrective measures when comprehension falters. Students with LD, however, do not often spontaneously engage in self-regulation. They can benefit from instruction in self-questioning strategies that rely on the principles as shown in the following box.

Principles for Self-Questioning Strategies

❏ Students are instructed how to generate questions and locate main ideas.

❏ Teachers model their own internal dialogues for students, and students practice these dialogues.

❏ Questions may reflect students' understanding about sections already read or may allow them to predict what is likely to occur.

❏ Teachers model main idea questions, which need to be paraphrased, and discourage detail questions, which can be lifted directly from the text.

❏ Questions require students to reflect on the purpose of the passage and encourage students to make informed predictions. (Raphael & Gavelek, 1984)

2. **Reciprocal Teaching—Grades 1–12.** Students engage in a dialogue about the text by sharing responsibility as group leader. After reading a portion of the text silently, the leader summarizes the information orally, asks a question of the group, helps to clarify information, and predicts what will happen next. The teacher participates as a member of the group by modeling use of the strategies through the course of the dialogue. He or she provides the degree of support needed by the group leader and can modify as needed for the students with learning difficulties (Palincsar, 1987). (For a complete description of reciprocal teaching see Appendix 2.)

3. **Skim, Rap, and Map—Grades 4–12** (developed by S. Taber, Institute for Learning and Development)

> *Skim* text by reading titles; headings and subheadings; captions under pictures; charts; maps; initial sentence of each paragraph; words in quotes, italics, or bold type; questions embedded in the text; introductions and summaries.

> *Rap* about a section by forming a question from the heading or topic sentence and locating the answer.

> *Map* by creating a two-column chart (dividing a page down the center), by placing rap questions in the left-hand

column, and by listing rap answers in the corresponding right-hand column. Students can self-quiz later and check their comprehension by covering the rap answers and asking themselves the rap questions.

4. **Marking Text—Grades 6–12**

Margin Notes: As students read silently, they interact with text by marking symbols in the margin to indicate their level of understanding. This activity draws students' attention to their own involvement in the process and improves self-monitoring.

- *Checkmark* confirms understanding ("Yes").

- *Question mark* indicates confusion or need for clarification ("Huh?").

- *Exclamation point* indicates amazement or surprise ("Wow!").

Highlighters—Grades 4–12: Teach students how to find main themes in texts and highlight these with a red marker: Use headings and subheadings to predict topics, locate topic sentences, identify key vocabulary words that label or classify information, find rules and generalizations. Teach strategies for locating details that support the main themes: Identify lists in a series, find examples of a rule, identify signal words for causal relationships (*because, since, as, for, hence, therefore, so, as a result*). Highlight supportive details with a yellow marker.

Post-It Notes: Students who are unable to write in their books or who have difficulty locating key pages may find use of Post-It Notes helpful. They can be used to highlight main ideas and details or monitor understanding as well as mark pages that contain central concepts.

5. **Backtracking—Grades 6–12.** When a breakdown in comprehension occurs, skilled readers often look back at text they have already read to clarify specific information. This strategy develops spontaneously in normal achievers during middle and high school years (Garner, 1987). However, students with LD who are unaware of their comprehension difficulties or are unfamiliar with the text structure may be less apt to use backtracking as a comprehension strategy (Paris & Winograd, 1990). Direct instruction in how and when to use this strategy has been effective with remedial readers (Garner, Hare, Alexander, Haynes, & Winograd, 1984).

6. **Semantic Mapping.** Semantic mapping involves the linking of verbal concepts in a visual presentation. Students focus on central themes and key vocabulary and "see" how these interrelate. Different maps can be used for different purposes. A vocabulary/concept map was introduced in the prereading section. Maps can also focus on the structure of text. Using these maps routinely helps students learn that selections from a specific genre are structured similarly. This is particularly helpful for students with learning disabilities who have good visual-spatial abilities, but exhibit weaknesses with prioritizing and language organization. Instruction that emphasizes these key components not only improves comprehension for students with learning disabilities, but also helps all students to focus on relevant themes. In addition, this knowledge can aid students' recall and provide a focal point for discussion.

> *Story Maps:* Key story components are presented in an appropriate semantic map. As a prereading activity, the title and first paragraph of the story are read. Students predict the story based on the questions posed on the map, and the predictions are recorded. During reading, the map is amended at critical points as predictions are confirmed and new predictions are made (Indrisano, 1984; see Figure 4.3).

> *Episode Webs:* Some stories are structured by a series of loosely related episodes rather than by an involved plot. These are often lighthearted, humorous stories that have high entertainment value. Instead of a story map, an episode web can be used to summarize each section (see Figure 4.4).

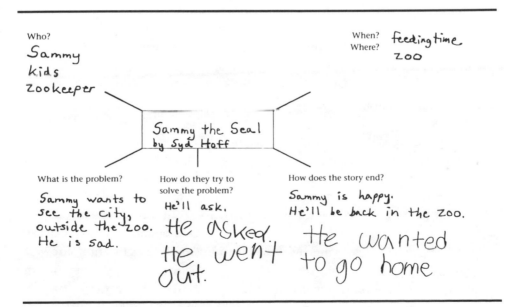

Figure 4.3. Example of a story map.

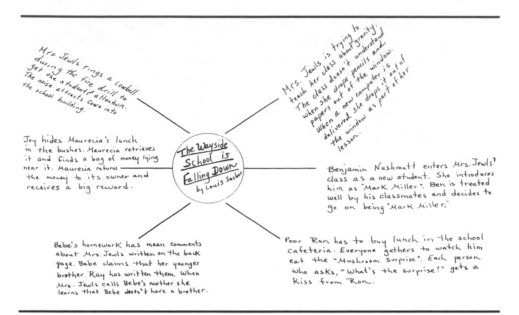

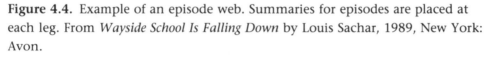

Figure 4.4. Example of an episode web. Summaries for episodes are placed at each leg. From *Wayside School Is Falling Down* by Louis Sachar, 1989, New York: Avon.

> *Expository Maps:* Factual, nonfiction texts do not follow a story structure, but rather are organized based on the concepts that are being presented. Maps are chosen according to the structure of the text and visually link concepts to text structure. As with the story map, use expository maps first as a prereading activity to activate prior knowledge and introduce new concepts. After reading all or parts of the text, use these maps as a postreading strategy to add or modify information based on the new information acquired through reading. Andrea, a seventh grader, created the expository map shown in Figure 4.5 from her social studies textbook (*Eastern Hemisphere*, Endsley, 1991).

7. **Imagery—Grades 4–12.** Many good readers make sense of text by forming mental images as they read. Imagery improves comprehension and memory by linking words with visual images and integrating parts of the text with the whole. Students with learning disabilities, particularly those with language-based difficulties, may not automatically visualize as they read but can develop this strategy through systematic instruction. Two programs have been developed with students with language-based learning disabilities in mind: the Wilson Success System (Wilson, 1992) and the *Visualizing and Verbalizing* program (Bell, 1991). These programs can be adapted for use within a heterogeneous classroom. Each of these programs emphasizes the following principles:

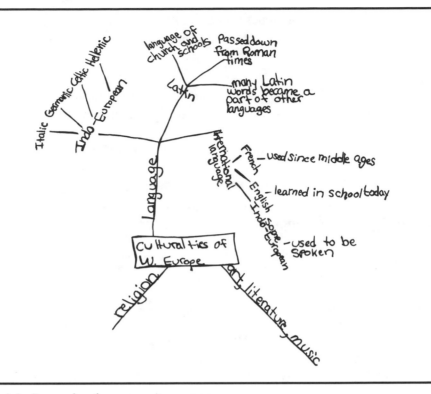

Figure 4.5. Example of an expository map.

- Start visualization training with familiar words or experiences. Instruct students to mentally "make a picture" or "make a movie." Ask specific questions to elicit detailed images (e.g., color, size, shape, etc.).

- Introduce short, concrete, descriptive passages at levels below students' grade placement. These are read to the student. As students develop proficiency, gradually add oral reading and silent reading of text. Later, increase the length and vary the subject matter.

- Use questioning to help students form images after each sentence. Questions should focus on attributes of the images (e.g., color, size, etc.) and serve to increase the amount of detail within the images. Gradually extend the length of text by discussing images after each paragraph, then after each page.

- Present model images and discuss these. When presenting models, the teacher acts as an active participant (e.g., "In my movie [picture] I saw . . .").

- Rehearse the visual sequence. In the Wilson system, students are instructed to "Rewind the film and watch it again." In *Visualizing and Verbalizing*, students give a sentence-by-sentence picture by describing, "Here I saw . . . " for each sentence (then paragraph).

- Formulate a verbal summary. The verbal summary should reflect an understanding of the main themes and how individual parts relate to the whole.

(*Note*: For a detailed description of these visualization training programs, please refer to the resources listed in the reference list at the end of this book.)

For a further discussion of note-taking, test-taking, and report-writing strategies, see Chapter 7.

••

D. Postreading Strategies

Postreading strategies can incorporate the following:

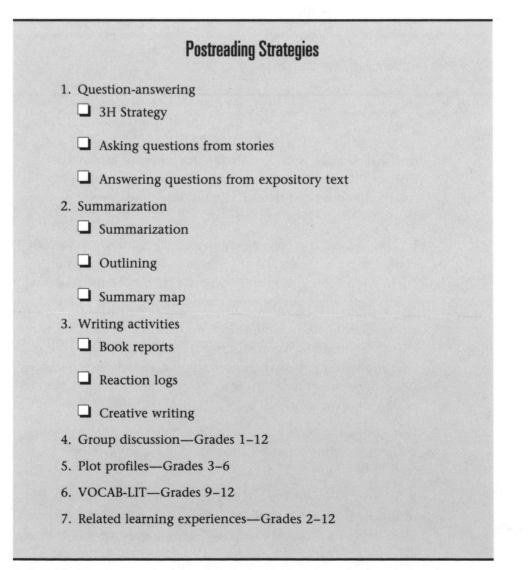

Postreading Strategies

1. Question-answering
   - ❑ 3H Strategy
   - ❑ Asking questions from stories
   - ❑ Answering questions from expository text
2. Summarization
   - ❑ Summarization
   - ❑ Outlining
   - ❑ Summary map
3. Writing activities
   - ❑ Book reports
   - ❑ Reaction logs
   - ❑ Creative writing
4. Group discussion—Grades 1–12
5. Plot profiles—Grades 3–6
6. VOCAB-LIT—Grades 9–12
7. Related learning experiences—Grades 2–12

Question-Answering

Reading curricula often use question-answering as a major component of compre-hension instruction. Following the reading of a selection, teachers ask students questions during discussion groups or students write answers to comprehension questions. How, then, can this activity be made more strategic so that students are learning about the processes involved in reading rather than merely being tested on their recall? What kinds of questions will enhance students' understanding of the text and level of involvement in the task?

Questions typically fall into one of three categories:

- Text explicit (located directly in the text)

- Text implicit (requires an inference by integrating information within the text)

- Script implicit (dependent on the reader's background knowledge or the reader's evaluation of the material)

Some students with LD may not readily recognize these types of questions, but sensitizing students to this information has been shown to improve the question-answering ability of average and low average readers. Various strategies have been effective in achieving this end; one is outlined below.

1. **The 3H Strategy—Grades 5–6.** Students are taught to use various "helpers" each time they answer a question from a text:

    - How will I answer this question?

    - Where is the answer to this question found?

        Here: The answer can be found in one sentence in the passage.

        Hidden: Use more than one idea from the passage to answer the question.

        In my head: Use what you already know. (Graham & Wong, 1993)

2. **Asking Questions About Stories—Grades 1–3.** Teachers may develop specific questions for each story based on the important features common to all stories. Questions may be as follows:

    - *Where* and *when* does the story take place? (setting)

    - *Who* are the characters? (protagonists)

    - *What* is the problem? (problem)

    - *Why* is this happening? (goal)

    - *How* is the problem resolved? (resolution) (Pearson, 1984)

For students with language-processing problems, rephrase question words routinely:

where = at what place

when = at what time (month, season, etc.)

who = which person, character

why = for what reason

how = in what way

With practice, this method can be developed into self-questioning procedures.

3. **Answering Questions from Expository Text—Grades 4–12**

Bloom's Taxonomy: Develop questions related to each level of learning. After modeling appropriate questions with students, have them develop questions and share these with classmates. These questions can become the basis for group discussion.

Knowledge (e.g., explain, list)

Comprehension (e.g., summarize, paraphrase)

Analysis (e.g., compare/contrast)

Synthesis (e.g., add new ideas, identify additional research)

Evaluation (e.g., form opinions, make judgments)

Self-questioning: Turn headings and subheadings into questions and review the material.

Summarization

It has been shown that most children, including students with learning difficulties, do not use summarization spontaneously or well (Pressley, 1988). Yet, summarization is an important technique. Children can be taught strategies to improve their summarization abilities in a number of ways.

1. **Summarization Rules—Grades 6–12.** Students are taught summarization rules and learn to apply them as follows:

- Delete trivial information.

- Delete redundant information.

- Substitute superordinate terms for lists of items.

- Integrate a series of events with a superordinate action term.

- Select a topic sentence or invent one if none is provided. (Kintsch & Van Dijk, 1978)

2. Outlining—Grades 6–12

> • Use headings, subheadings, and paragraphs to develop an outline of text.
>
> • Generate main idea statements for every heading, subheading, and paragraph.

3. **Summary Map—Grades 2–12.** Create a semantic map that highlights main themes. Use "webbing" by placing the title in the middle with four to six main ideas from the reading listed in a circle around the title. This web can be used for subsequent writing or studying. (See Figure 4.4 on page 48 for an example.)

Writing Activities

1. **Book Reports—Grades 2–12.** Writing a book report is a popular postreading activity in which students frequently engage. How can this activity enhance strategic learning?

> • Before the reading begins, determine which strategies students will need and what the focus of the report will be. Will students be required to summarize? evaluate? make inferences? answer questions? Will the focus be on characterization? setting? plot?
>
> • Teach *prereading* and *active reading* strategies that are relevant to the focus of the book report.
>
> • Discuss with the students the focus of the book report *before* reading. Consider how this affects purposes students set for reading.
>
> • Teach additional procedural skills that students will need to complete the report (e.g., how to locate author, publisher, copyright date, and full references).
>
> • Try different formats (e.g., newspaper, cartoons, locating textual evidence that supports the title).

2. **Reaction Logs.** Students maintain a journal with their reactions and comments. Responses are discussed in groups. Possible formats are as follows:

Fiction

Literature log—Grades 4–8: Students keep a record of the pages they have read and make comments about the reading. The teacher can structure these comments for students with learning difficulties by providing sentence starters (e.g., "I predict this will happen next . . .").

Dialogue journal—Grades 4–12: Through writing, students and the teacher discuss their books and the strategies they use while reading. The student writes his or her comments in the journal. The teacher responds to the student by writing comments that help the student to further explore his or her thoughts. The student is encouraged to focus on strategies (e.g., making predictions, asking questions, requesting clarification, making evaluations) and literary elements (e.g., leads, exploration of genre or theme, figurative language, author's style). Dialogue journals can also be completed with peers (Atwell, 1987; see Figure 4.6).

Nonfiction

Learning log—Grades 1–8: After reading in the content areas, students record new concepts they have learned. In Grades 1 through 3, students select a few new facts they have learned, write a sentence for each fact, and illustrate. In Grades 4 through 8, students write paragraphs about the concepts and draw diagrams or charts to illustrate these. They can develop questions from sub-headings and relate their paragraphs to these questions.

Reaction log using two-column format—Grades 9–12

Text	Reaction
In this column, record section of text that has caused you to react in some way.	In this column, record your reactions. • Do you have relevant personal experiences that have caused you to react in a certain way? • Has this raised questions? • How will you attempt to answer these? • What issues would you raise with the author if given the opportunity?

3. **Creative Writing—Grades 7–12.** Additional writing activities may branch off reading themes. As with book reports, choose those activities that enhance the strategies learned during the reading.

Fiction

Write new endings: Students alter some of the facts before the resolution and rewrite the endings. Or, write a prologue or epilogue.

Write alternate viewpoints: Students rewrite the story according to another character's viewpoint. Or, letters or journal entries can be written from the points of view of different characters.

Create an original story: Outline a new story using the semantic map by having each student enter original characters, settings, and plot summaries before writing

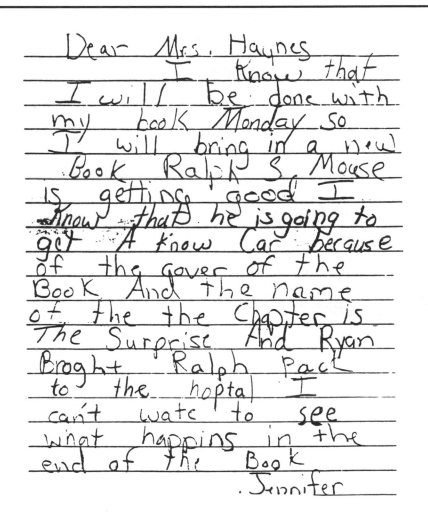

Dear Mrs. Haynes
        I Know that
I will be done with
my book Monday so
I will bring in a new
Book Ralph S. Mouse
is getting good I
Know that he is going to
get A know Car because
of the gover of the
Book And the name
of the the Chapter is
The Surprise And Ryan
Broght Ralph Pack
to the hoptal I
can't wate to see
what happins in the
end of the Book
                    Jennifer

October 27, 1989

Dear Jennifer,
        You are showing me another
strategy that you have learned. Readers
predict what they think will happen
next. You have predicted what will
happen to Ralph S. Mouse at the end
of the book. Let me know if your
prediction is correct in your next
letter. Please remember your date.
                    Mrs. Haynes

Figure 4.6. Example of a dialogue journal.

the story. Stories could be written in the same genre (e.g., action/adventure, mystery) to develop awareness of the characteristics of the genre. For stories that are episodic, write a new episode.

Nonfiction

Newspaper articles: Students use facts in the reading to develop newspaper articles that explore the issues from a particular angle. Students with learning difficulties may benefit from using a list of *wh-* question words to focus their ideas and to organize their writing (i.e., *who, what, when, where, why*).

Interviews: Students create mock interviews with famous people from the reading and use information in the text as the basis for their questions and answers. Or, students conduct actual interviews with people who are knowledgeable about the subject (e.g., when studying the early 20th century, interview elderly people in area nursing homes). Students with learning difficulties may need a structured approach to develop appropriate interview questions.

Persuasive essay: Students use facts from reading to support a particular viewpoint. Provide models of persuasive essays to illustrate the structure.

Report writing: See suggestions in Chapter 7.

Group Discussion—Grades 1–12

Teachers and students engage in a dialogue about the literature rather than a question–answer session with the teacher in control. In this way, the teacher becomes a participant and a model. Students recognize that their thoughts and opinions are valued and that they are not being tested to see if they "got it right." Competition is reduced, and even reticent participants can contribute. Discussion can focus on the following topics:

Characters: Their key roles, the ways in which they develop throughout the course of the book, their appeal to the readers.

Plot: The main events, the significance of these events, the readers' predictions and reactions from these events. For some stories, a plot profile can be completed.

Plot Profiles—Grades 3–6

Students summarize and evaluate the plot of a well-structured story. (These are especially useful with action/adventure stories or mysteries.)

- In small groups, students summarize the main events of the story and list them in sequence on the chart.

- Students collectively discuss the level of excitement they felt for each event and rate this on a 10-point scale.

- Points are plotted on the graph to illustrate student reactions using a plot profile similar to that developed by Butler (1988) (see Figure 4.7).

Setting: Readers' visualization of the setting and the language in the text that contributed to this

Author's style: How the author *shows* meaning rather than *tells* it, the author's background and how this contributed to the story, the mood the author created

Theme: The author's purpose for writing it, the message conveyed, other books with similar themes, similar experiences students may have had.

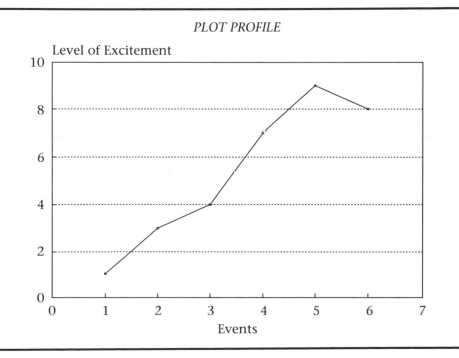

Figure 4.7. Example of a plot profile.

VOCAB-LIT—Grades 9–12

As a postreading strategy, VOCAB-LIT reinforces concepts in the text and extends students' vocabulary knowledge (Chase & Duffelmeyer, 1990).

- Following a reading assignment, the teacher chooses a word from the reading that is conceptually important to the major themes in the text.
- Using the form in Figure 4.8, students individually indicate their familiarity with the word.
- As a group, students share prior knowledge of the word.
- On the form, students copy the sentence from the text in which the word occurred. Then, the group discusses the meaning of the word based on this context.
- Students locate the word in the dictionary and copy the appropriate definition.
- Students discuss how knowledge of the word has enhanced their understanding of the text (e.g., specific literary element, concept, or theme).
- Each student is assigned a day to present a word to the group from the previous day's reading assignment. The teacher facilitates this process and assists as needed.

Related Learning Experiences—Grades 2–12

1. **Comparison/Contrast.** Various learning experiences related to the themes in the reading can be used to extend students' understanding of concepts, including filmstrips, movies, tape recordings, demonstrations, discussions, lectures,

Word:	<u>My Knowledge</u>	<u>Group Strategy</u>
☐	Unknown ☐	Discussion ☐
	Familiar ☐	Context ☐
	Well-Known ☐	Dictionary ☐

Context Sentence: ____________________

Definition: ____________________

What's Learned: ____________________

Figure 4.8. Example of a VOCAB-LIT card.

and additional readings. This new information is linked to the reading by adding information to previous maps or outlines or by comparing/contrasting sources of information.

> *Comparison/contrast map:* Students compare and contrast sources of information on a Venn diagram (see Appendix 3). For example, events in a particular book can be contrasted with the movie version.

> *Comparison/contrast matrix:* After reading/viewing several versions of the same story, or several presentations of the same theme, students compare and contrast the versions using the chart in Figure 4.9.

2. **Related Projects.** Various projects can be undertaken that extend understanding of the concepts in the text. Students can choose the method of presentation that capitalizes on their strengths. Some examples are listed on the next page.

	Version 1	Version 2	Version 3	Alike	Different	Conclusions
Title	"The Little Boy's Secret"	"The Giant Who Threw Tantrums"	"The Giant Who Was Afraid of Butterflies"			
Setting	woods & giant's castle	village & woods	valley & hill	Each story takes place "long ago."		Stories take place where there is a lot of space for giants to roam.
Characters	Little boy, 3 nasty giants	Little boy, kind giant, foolish villagers	Little boy, friendly giant, mean witch	In 2 & 3, boy & giant are friends.	The bad guy is different in each one.	Sometimes unlikely friendships can occur.
Problem	The boy is kidnapped by giants because he won't tell his secret.	The giant throws tantrums because he can't whistle.	The witch puts spell on the giant.		In each of the stories the conflict is caused by different characters.	Where there are giants & witches you can expect trouble!
Events	The boy tells each giant his secret & they run away frightened	The villagers hear noises but don't believe they are caused by a giant, even when the boy sees the giant.	The witch casts a spell and the giant sees things as twice his size. The boy gets the giant eyeglasses, which return his sight to normal.			In each story the boy is much wiser than the giant.
Ending	The boy breaks out in measels, revealing his secret.	The boy teaches the giant to whistle. Now the villagers hear whistling off in the distance.	The giant and boy scold the witch and go off to play.			Ongoing friendships between boys & giants are rare.

Figure 4.9. Compare/contrast matrix for three stories. Stories compiled from *The Book of Giant Stories* by David Harrison, 1972, New York: American Heritage Press.

Models, maps, dioramas: Good for students with strengths in visual-spatial skills, part–whole relationships, fine motor skills.

Time lines, cartoon strips, filmstrips: Good for students with temporal–sequential strengths.

Travel brochures, photographs, drawings, posters: Good for students with artistic abilities.

Role-playing, debates, oral presentations: Good for students with oral language strengths.

E. Expanding Vocabulary Knowledge

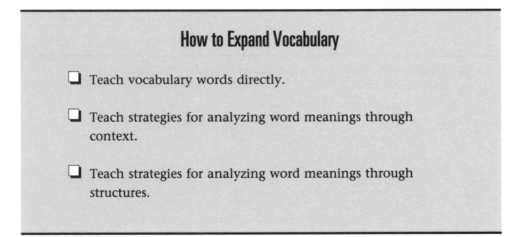

How to Expand Vocabulary

❏ Teach vocabulary words directly.

❏ Teach strategies for analyzing word meanings through context.

❏ Teach strategies for analyzing word meanings through structures.

As students learn new vocabulary, individual word banks are compiled that consist of words students collect through the course of a year or over a period of years. These words can be referred to and used during reading and writing activities. This enriches students' vocabulary usage and helps them develop strategies and awareness of the processes they use when learning new words.

Teaching Vocabulary Words Directly

Research has shown that students with weaknesses in vocabulary not only know fewer words than their more skilled peers, but have limited knowledge about the words they know, because much of their word knowledge is bound to a particular context (Curtis, 1987). Direct methods of instruction have been shown to be effective in improving the quality of vocabulary knowledge for skilled and less skilled readers (Chall, 1987; Curtis, 1986; Johnson & Pearson, 1978). Students with learning disabilities remember new vocabulary best when using methods that use mnemonic (memory) aids and relate new words to prior knowledge (Mastropieri, Scruggs, & Levin, 1985; Roswell & Natchez, 1977).

1. **Key Word Method.** Students who have difficulty remembering definitions of new words may benefit from this mnemonic strategy, which has been shown to be particularly effective among students with learning disabilities (Mastropieri et al., 1985). It incorporates the following principles:

   - *Recording:* Students choose a key word that sounds similar to the target word.

   - *Relating:* The recorded word is related to the target word's meaning through a picture.

   - *Retrieving:* The student thinks of the picture, associates this with the key word, and in turn remembers the target word.

   Students' key words and interactive pictures can be recorded on index cards and added to individual word banks. Sentences that contain both the target word and the key word can be developed to further illustrate the definition. Stephanie, a high school senior, developed the key word shown in Figure 4.10 for the word *belligerence.*

2. **Word Wheels—Grades 1–12.** Develop a synonym (or antonym or homonym) web by placing the main vocabulary word inside a bubble in the center of the page or index card. Related synonyms, antonyms, or homonyms are placed in surrounding bubbles and connected to the main word with "spokes."

3. **Semantic Feature Analysis—Grades 4–12**

   - Words that share certain features are selected from the reading lesson, content area topic, or individual word banks. These are listed in a column on a chalkboard or piece of paper.

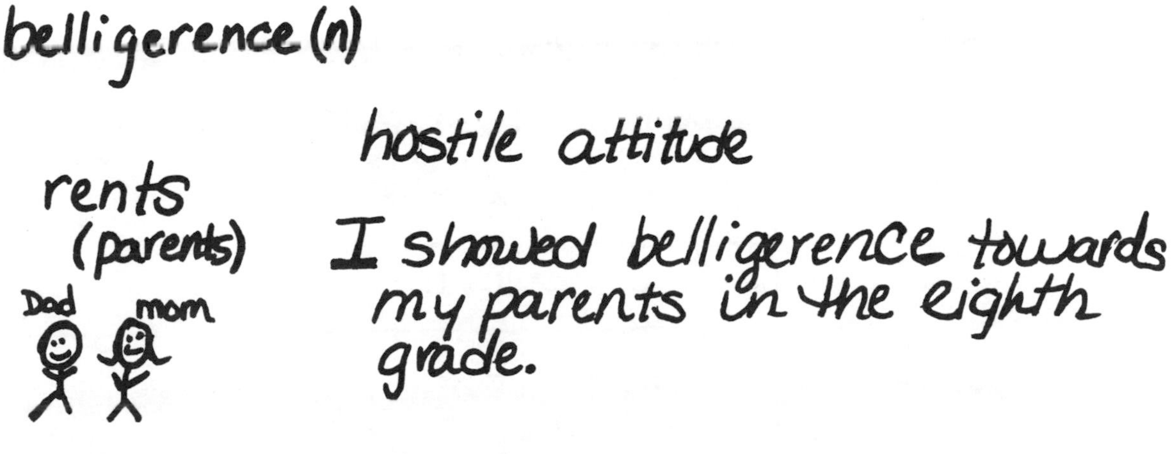

Figure 4.10. Mnemonic strategy for recalling terminology and concepts: key word for the word *belligerence.*

- Students generate features that at least one of the words possesses. These words are listed in rows across the top of the board or paper thus forming a matrix.

- Students assign plus or minus values to words and features. As students become more proficient, scales of numbers could replace plus and minus values to indicate varying degrees of features.

- After completing the grid, students can add more words and features to the grid.

- Through discussion, students discover the uniqueness of words, because no two words will have the same identical pattern of pluses or minuses.

- Discussion of features should teach students new words as well as expand their understanding of words they know.

- As words and features are conceptually related but cut across grammatical categories, students can then write sentences and paragraphs using words and features in the grid. This process is called *semantic feature analysis* and was developed by Anders, Bos, and Filip (1984). The grid shown in Figure 4.11 was developed with a fifth grader using vocabulary from his word bank.

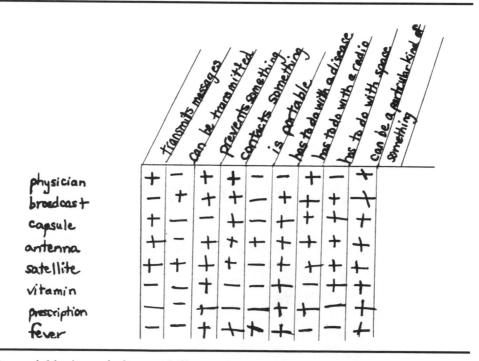

Figure 4.11. A vocabulary grid illustrating semantic feature analysis.

Teaching Strategies for Analyzing Word Meanings Through Context

Despite the advantages of direct vocabulary instruction, these methods can teach students only a limited number of words. Students also need to develop strategies for using context clues to discern word meanings. Skilled readers acquire most of their vocabulary knowledge through reading connected text (Nagy, Herman, & Anderson, 1985). Students with learning disabilities, however, often read less than their skilled peers and may lack sufficient exposure to words in context. Also, they often have difficulty inferring word meanings through context. They can, however, develop effective strategies for using context to learn word meanings in order to maximize their reading experiences. Some of those strategies are listed below.

Effective Strategies for Using Context to Learn Word Meanings

❏ Provide sentences with rich context (i.e., many clues about the word's meaning) and weak context (i.e., few clues about the word's meaning).

❏ Provide passages that contain the words in a variety of contexts. Or, for each word develop a list of 7 to 10 sentences that provide clues to the meaning of the word.

❏ Use various cues to infer meanings of the words, including category membership, physical properties of the word, and the importance of the word's meaning to understanding the text (Curtis, 1986).

❏ Provide opportunities for students to write the words in their own contexts.

❏ Students practice this strategy during silent reading times.

❏ Unknown words are recorded on index cards along with the sentences in which they were found and possible definitions. The words can be added to individual word banks.

Teaching Strategies for Analyzing Word Meanings Through Structure

Students can be taught to identify structural components in words (prefixes, suffixes, and root words) and use this information to figure out the meanings of new words.

1. Structural Methods for Elementary Students—Grades 2–5

- Teach the meanings of common prefixes and suffixes that occur frequently and have consistent meanings: negation prefixes (*un-, in-, dis-, non-*) *com-, ex-, pre-, re-, sub-, -tion, -ment, -ful, -less* (Roswell & Natchez, 1977).

- Begin with familiar root words.

- Use a step-by-step procedure with students who have difficulty with analysis/synthesis (Durkin, 1976):

  —*Analyze:* Determine if word contains affix(es).

  —*Dismantle:* Remove prefixes first, then suffixes.

  —*Identify:* Identify and define root word.

  —*Reassemble:* Reattach suffixes first, then prefixes, and discuss changes in meaning as each affix is added.

2. Structural Methods for Secondary Students—Grades 6–12

- Teach affixes and roots that carry clear, consistent meaning, occur frequently, and can be used to identify the word's meaning. For example, the suffix *-ty* occurs frequently and consistently, but its meaning is unclear and does little to add to an understanding of the word.

- Selection of specific affixes and roots depends on the needs of the learner. Determine whether there is a need to teach non-English roots and decide which roots are appropriate to teach based on reading demands and student goals. For example, college bound students may need more extensive training than non-college bound students.

- Teach meanings of affixes and roots by using words that were already in student's vocabulary. For example, teach *-cracy* through *democracy*, then add new word *theocracy* (O'Rourke, 1974).

- Develop an ongoing vocabulary file with each student. Create a holistic perspective of each new word by including the part of speech, a mnemonic aid, and a descriptive sentence using the word and, if possible, its meaning or partial clue.

It is a challenging task to meet the range of reading needs within the heterogeneous classroom. Yet, many activities can benefit *all* students, not just those students with learning difficulties. We hope this section has given you a few new ideas. Remember, change is gradual. Think big, but start small. Select a new strategy and incorporate it into a series of lessons. When you feel comfortable with this, try something new. Here are a few questions you need to ask before planning instruction:

What Questions You Need to Ask Before Planning Instruction

❏ What processes does this particular task require?

❏ What strategies do I need to teach all students based on the demand of this task?

❏ What modifications do I need to make for individual students who may need additional support?

How might you use these strategies during a reading lesson? Imagine for a minute that you are a fourth-grade teacher who is teaching a literature group. You have eight students in your group, three of whom have learning problems. You have chosen the text *Trouble River* by Betsy Byars (1984), because it is fast-paced and uses understandable language. This is a story about a pioneer boy and his grandmother who vacate their cabin to escape hostile Indians. Their only chance for survival is to travel downstream on a raft to join the boy's parents in a neighboring town. Your activities may be similar to those shown in Table 4.2.

Table 4.2. How Instruction Can Be Individualized to Promote Reading Comprehension

Group	Sara	Bill	Tom
Eight students; heterogeneous, flexible groups; focus on reading comprehension, action/adventure genre, sequential organization	LD; processing skills are strong in visual channel, weak in language	LD; good comprehender, poor decoder	ADD; overfocuses on details
Activate Students' Prior Knowledge			
Discuss early pioneers and the dangers they encountered.	Provide pictures of early pioneers. Speak slowly. Allow extra time to process information and responses.	Assume he will follow general discussion.	Provide preferential seating. Make frequent eye contact. Provide pictures of early pioneers.

(continued)

Table 4.2. (*Continued*)

Group	Sara	Bill	Tom
Review Vocabulary			
Present words in sentences that have many context clues. Students write possible definitions for the words. Students volunteer definitions, which are recorded on a class chart.	Discussion of how to use context clues is critical to Sara's understanding of this strategy.	Assist with word identification. Bill should syllabicate and decode words. Use these words in Bill's decoding and spelling lessons.	Check that Tom has grasped the directions and remains on task.
Reciprocal Teaching			
Read first few pages silently as a group to identify lead, major characters, setting, basic problem in plot. Change group leaders at natural break points. Facilitate and model appropriate strategy use.			Have Tom mark predetermined break points.
Semantic Mapping			
Using a variation of the story map to accommodate the episodic subplots that occur.	The visual representation of the map is critical for Sara. Rephrase questions about the setting, such as "At what time?" and "In what place?" because Sara often confuses where/when.		
Silent Reading			
Provide quiet time for sections of the story to be read silently. Students record reactions in literature logs and bring to group discussions.		Pair Bill and Tom to read orally in a quiet section of the room. Each assumes the responsibility of "tutoring" the other. Tom assists Bill with decoding difficult, multisyllabic words.	Bill helps Tom remain on task.

(*continued*)

Table 4.2. (*Continued*)

Group	Sara	Bill	Tom
Group Discussion			
Make and confirm predictions using the map. Discuss students' reactions from logs, including those regarding strategy use. Amend vocabulary chart to reflect increased understanding of the words as they are encountered in text. Add words to individual word banks.	Allow extra time to process information and formulate responses. Group discussion is critical for Sara to learn word meanings as well as to learn strategies for unlocking word meanings through context.		Mapping is critical for Tom, who has difficulty prioritizing details and identifying main themes.
Plot Profile			
After story is completed, students analyze how subplots relate to the larger plot. Help students make judgments and negotiate responses.	Profile provides visual representation of plot. Sara develops understanding of sequence.	Profile helps Bill to develop part–whole relationships.	Profile helps Tom to prioritize details and to integrate these with the main theme.

During this lesson, each student has developed a unique repertoire of active reading strategies. Although students may have reached different levels of understanding of the book, development has proceeded at an appropriate pace in a manner conducive to each student's learning style.

Chapter 5

Strategies for Enhancing Written Language

In this chapter we discuss the important components of written language and ways you can help your students become better writers.

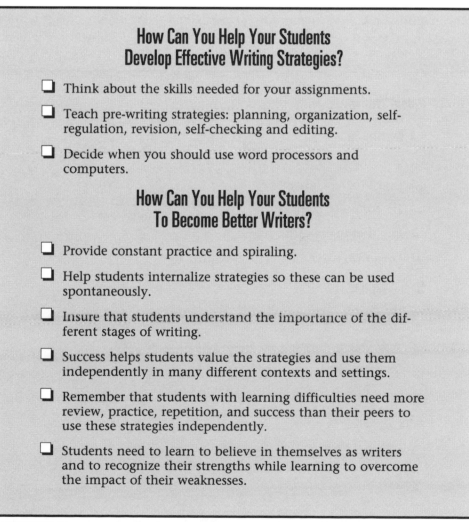

How Can You Help Your Students Develop Effective Writing Strategies?

❑ Think about the skills needed for your assignments.

❑ Teach pre-writing strategies: planning, organization, self-regulation, revision, self-checking and editing.

❑ Decide when you should use word processors and computers.

How Can You Help Your Students To Become Better Writers?

❑ Provide constant practice and spiraling.

❑ Help students internalize strategies so these can be used spontaneously.

❑ Insure that students understand the importance of the different stages of writing.

❑ Success helps students value the strategies and use them independently in many different contexts and settings.

❑ Remember that students with learning difficulties need more review, practice, repetition, and success than their peers to use these strategies independently.

❑ Students need to learn to believe in themselves as writers and to recognize their strengths while learning to overcome the impact of their weaknesses.

Why Teach Strategies in Writing?

Writing instruction has historically focused on the final products of writing. Teachers frequently assigned topics, graded papers, made corrections, and returned these to students. The belief was that students would internalize the teacher's comments (if they read them at all!) and generalize these to the next composition. In addition, exercises in grammar were completed and graded; knowing *what* a sentence consisted of was believed to teach students *how* to write.

Even though writing is an activity that challenges all students, little time has actually been spent on teaching students the process of writing. Similarly, students have been rarely been allotted classroom time for sustained writing. Text production skills have received most of the attention in writing instruction (i.e., handwriting, spelling, sentence structure), despite research indicating that traditional grammar instruction does *not* improve students' writing (Hillocks, 1986). Little attention has been given to higher level thought processes, including planning, revising, and self-regulation. Yet, these are important components of writing. The writing process is similar to the reading process and includes several components:

Before Writing

❑ Setting goals

❑ Generating ideas (e.g., brainstorming)

❑ Considering audience

❑ Determining point of view

❑ Identifying main themes

❑ Organizing ideas in a logical sequence

During Writing

❑ Prioritizing

❑ Selecting appropriate language to match thought

❑ Applying strategies flexibly

❑ Coordinating multiple subskills and processes

After Writing

❑ Evaluating

❑ Revising

❑ Editing

❑ Applying outside standards of correctness (adapted from Squire, 1984)

Skilled writers move in and out of these stages spontaneously rather than following them in a linear fashion. For example, editing for spelling or punctuation errors may occur while writing. However, when writing is complete, editing may occur again using a more systematic approach (see Table 5.1).

How Can You Help Students Develop Writing Strategies?

You can help your students develop writing strategies in the following ways:

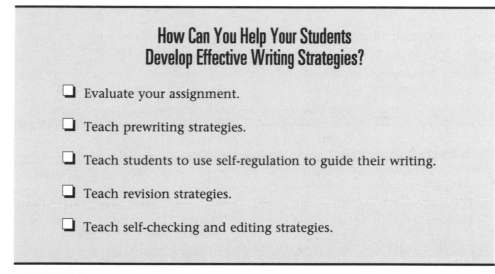

How Can You Help Your Students Develop Effective Writing Strategies?

❑ Evaluate your assignment.

❑ Teach prewriting strategies.

❑ Teach students to use self-regulation to guide their writing.

❑ Teach revision strategies.

❑ Teach self-checking and editing strategies.

Evaluate Your Assignments: Which Strategies Will Students Need?

- How will the writing be structured?

- Is research or note-taking required?

- What is the focus of the assignment?

- Am I emphasizing creativity or attention to form?

- Will students need to develop a point of view?

- Do I expect a retelling of content or student interpretations?

- Have I clearly articulated the goals of the assignment to the students?

- Have these goals been clearly understood?

- Have I determined individual needs and planned instruction accordingly?

Table 5.1. A Comparison of Skilled Writers with Writers Who Have Difficulties

Skilled writers . . .	Students with writing difficulties . . .
• plan an approach.	• may have limited knowledge about the subject or have difficulty assessing their background information.
• formulate main themes and develop these with supportive details.	• may have difficulty identifying main themes and sticking to the topic.
• organize ideas in a logical sequence.	• may have limited understanding of text structures.
• write and revise their ideas.	• may display limited writing fluency and are reluctant to revise ideas or return to their writing.
• edit for spelling, capitalization, punctuation.	• may not easily recognize their errors or know how to correct them.
• monitor thought processes and devise solutions to problems they encounter.	• may be unaware of the strategies they are using or the strategies they need.
• demonstrate proficiency in numerous subskills and processes, including those related to motor demands (letter formation, fluency, spatial organization), form (spelling, grammar, mechanics), and content (vocabulary, organization, ideas).	• may have weaknesses in handwriting, spatial organization, and spelling that can impede their performance on higher level components of the writing process.
• coordinate multiple subskills as well as know when and how to use them.	• may have trouble integrating numerous subskills or have difficulty shifting strategies when needed.
• often generalize writing principles from reading (e.g., genre, language usage, sentence structures).	• often have limited experiences with reading and do not generalize principles to writing.

© 1996 PRO-ED, Inc.

Teach Prewriting Strategies

Goal-Setting.   Teacher and students work together to set goals for the paper and create a list of these goals. Goals may consider the following points (adapted from Harris & Graham, 1992):

What is the general purpose of the paper?

to inform
to entertain
to persuade
to compare/contrast
to retell
to present possibilities
to answer

What is the general structure of the paper?

> story format/genre
> main ideas/details
> comparison/contrast

Where can students find sources of information?

> personal experience
> background knowledge
> interviews
> class lecture
> textbooks
> additional research

What are the expectations regarding specific writing skills?
Which will be emphasized?

> vocabulary
> sentence structure
> spelling
> handwriting
> capitalization/punctuation

What are the expectations regarding length, format, due dates?

Securing Ideas

Brainstorming—Top-Down Versus Bottom-Up: Individualized brainstorming procedures could be used to accommodate students' learning styles. Students who demonstrate conceptual strengths could use a "top-down" procedure whereby they first identify main ideas and themes and then generate relevant, supporting details. Students who overfocus on details at the expense of the "big picture" could use a "bottom-up" procedure whereby they first brainstorm critical vocabulary and details and then prioritize and organize these details (see Figure 5.1).

Free Writing: During free writing, students write anything that comes to mind as fast as they can. They let their ideas flow without passing judgment on them. Then, they decide if any of these ideas have led them in a direction they wish to pursue further. For students who have difficulty with writing fluency, this activity can be made more gamelike through use of a "composition derby." The students and teacher free-write for a designated amount of time (2 to 5 minutes) and do not stop writing until time is called. Each student adds up the number of words written, and a total class score is computed and graphed for that day. (Or, two teams can be formed.) Over time, class output should increase as fluency improves. Students can keep individual graphs and retain compositions for further development of ideas. This activity is particularly helpful for the student with LD who has difficulty with writing fluency (Rhodes & Dudley-Marling, 1988).

Top-Down Writing Sample

If I were a shoe what would my life be like?

4/5/94

Description
Smelling
hot, sweaty
dirty
white
~~black~~ brown
big, small

Experiences
Stepped on
going everywhere
trips
vacations
around town, malls
School (etc.)

feelings
uncomfortable
hot
grose
broken in
comfortable

Getting worn out
getting dirty
getting holes
thrown away
worn everywhere
years of use.

If I were a shoe, I would look much different than I ~~it~~ do as a person. As a new shoe, I would be very white with other very distinct colors, but as I got ~~dirty~~ older and I was worn out and sweaty my color probaley would change to brown dirt. Also as I got older I would not be as ~~white and~~ stiff and clean. Along with my color changing ~~a~~ I would start to smell ~~bad~~ and get very hot and sticky. But the dirtier and smellier I got, the more broken in and comfortable I would be.

Bottom-Up Writing Sample

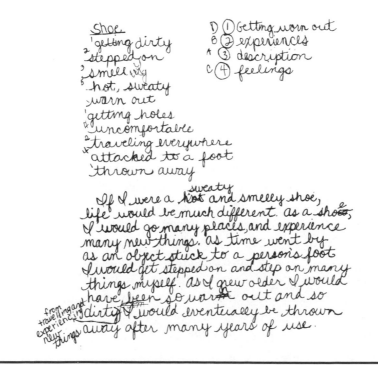

shoe
getting dirty
stepped on
smelly
hot, sweaty
worn out
getting holes
uncomfortable
traveling everywhere
attacked to a foot
thrown away

D ① Getting worn out
B ② experiences
A ③ description
C ④ feelings

If I were a ~~hot~~ sweaty and smelly shoe, life would be much different. As a shoe, I would go many places, and experience many new things. As time went by as an object stuck to a person's foot I would get stepped on and step on many things myself. As I grew older I would have ~~been~~ so worn out and so ~~from traveling and experiencing new things~~ dirty I would eventually be thrown away after many years of use.

Figure 5.1. Examples of top-down and bottom-up prewriting.

Individualized Topic Selection: The most complete sources of knowledge for students come from their own personal experiences. These experiences can be tapped to give students meaningful topics about which to write. Yet, many students, including students with learning disabilities, have difficulty accessing this information. Certain topic selection activities may help them discover the knowledge they have.

Younger students can use the "mining for topics" activity shown in Appendix 4 to help them formulate ideas. Teachers ask students questions that help them elicit knowledge they have. Sample questions are provided in Appendix 4. Students list their ideas vertically, close together, to accommodate an increasing topic selection list.

Older students can create an "authority inventory" whereby they each make a list of subjects in which they believe they are experts, including extracurricular activities, interests and hobbies, places they have lived or visited, people they know, family background, things they have done (Murray, 1984).

Research Methods: Students initially set purposes for writing and brainstorm their prior knowledge and point of view using the appropriate brainstorming procedure. Teachers can show students how to locate sources for their paper, and how to choose appropriate active reading and note-taking strategies. Help students find the system that works best for them. Demonstrate how to color-code note cards to correspond with specific sources. Research has indicated that, despite the emphasis on note-taking and outlining skills, very few student writers make use of those techniques (Hillocks, 1986).

For additional strategies, refer to Chapter 7.

Organizing Ideas

Understanding Text Structures: Develop concept of text structure through reading activities (see Chapter 4).

Cognitive Strategy Instruction in Writing Program (Englert, 1992): Teachers use student-authored texts to model strategies for recognizing text structures. The teacher initially guides the students through this process when introducing each type of writing. For example, when introducing comparison/contrast, the teacher might ask, "What is being compared/contrasted? How are they alike? How are they different?" Key words that signal this purpose are identified (e.g., *in contrast to, like, different*), and several writing samples, from well-written to poorly written, are used. After students have developed awareness of various structures, the teacher allows students to assume more of the dialogue by being less specific (e.g., "What kind of paper is this? How do you know?") (Englert, 1992).

Semantic Mapping: Once students have an understanding of basic text structures, students with strong visual-spatial skills can choose appropriate semantic maps to organize their writing (see Chapter 4). Using the brainstorming list, students group concepts together on the appropriate map. Figure 5.2 shows two examples from middle school students.

Outlining: Students who have strengths in language with weaknesses in visual-spatial skills may benefit from learning systematic outlining procedures or using index cards to organize their ideas. When introducing a new organizational

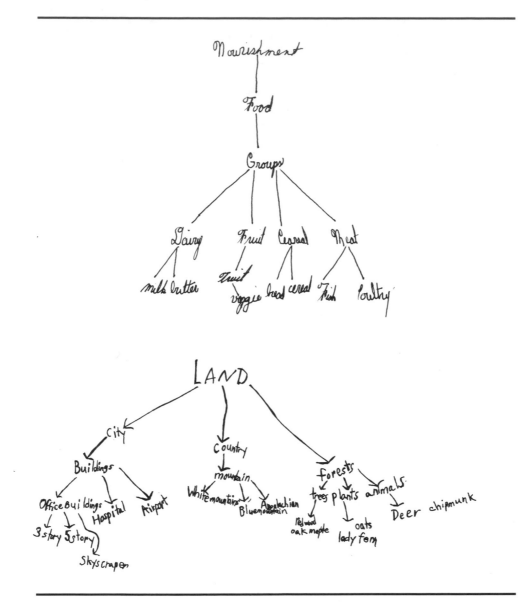

Figure 5.2. Two examples of semantic mapping.

system for writing or note-taking, provide a partially completed outline that allows students to fill in missing information. Decrease prompts for students who gain proficiency.

Teach Students to Use Self-Regulation to Guide Their Writing

During the composing process, students need to coordinate multiple subskills, processes, and strategies. Skilled writers use self-regulation to accomplish this purpose. Often, they talk to themselves while they write and give themselves verbal instructions as they go. Teachers can enhance students' use of self-talk by modeling their own self-instructions while writing. Harris and Graham (1992) described the following steps for teaching students how to use self-instructions in the context of strategy instruction.

- When introducing a new strategy, the teacher first describes the strategy in detail. The teacher and students discuss why, how, and when to use it.

- The teacher models the strategy while writing and uses appropriate self-talk during the process. These self-instructions can serve a number of purposes:

    —to identify problems as they are encountered (e.g., "What do I have to do here?")

    —to engage a particular strategy to solve the problem (e.g., "First, I will brainstorm ideas.")

    —to self-evaluate and self-correct when necessary (e.g., "Have I included all the parts to the story?")

    —to cope with frustrations (e.g., "I can handle this.")

    —to provide rewards (e.g., "I used great describing words.")

- The teacher and students discuss the types of self-instructions used during the modeling.

- Each student creates his or her own list of self-instructions, using teacher examples and the student's own ideas.

- Students memorize examples from their personal self-instructions lists.

- The teacher prompts students to use these self-instructions in various contexts until they become more automatic.

- Students employ the target strategy and self-instructions as they write. The teacher offers support and assistance as needed. Over time, strategies are combined and self-regulation is expanded.

Teach Revision Strategies

Analyzing Students' Writing

Conferencing: Conferences can be held regularly with the teacher, a peer, or through "self-conferences" in which students ask themselves questions. These conferences provide verbal feedback about the students' writing and focus on the ideas rather than the mechanics. Involving peers in conferencing activities helps students see the importance of writing for a variety of audiences. The feedback fellow classmates provide encourages students to improve the clarity and level of detail in their writing. Students can read their writing aloud or have peers read it independently.

Three basic components can be included in each conference:

- *Tell back:* The teacher/peer summarizes the student's content to determine if the reader's interpretation matches the writer's intended message.

- *Provide positive feedback:* The teacher reinforces appropriate use of strategies and skills. A peer discusses what he or she liked best about the writing. Writers with learning disabilities frequently exhibit negative attitudes toward their writing and lack confidence in their abilities. It is critical to provide positive feedback to these students about any skills and strategies used correctly or any improvements made, no matter how slight.

- *Provide constructive feedback:* The teacher teaches one or two new strategies or skills after discussing with the student which strategy or skill is needed to enhance the quality of the paper. For students with significant writing weaknesses, focus on errors that frequently occur. The student records the new strategy or skill on a procedural checklist or into a strategy notebook. A peer provides feedback regarding what he or she needs to have clarified in the writing.

- The teacher maintains a record of the conference.

Create sets of Criteria/Scales: Students analyze model pieces of writing and develop sets of criteria that illustrate certain characteristics in the writing. Rating scales can be developed based on the criteria. Students apply these criteria to their writing and the writing of others. They identify ways to improve the writing and suggest revisions. Studies have indicated that use of criteria and scales was not only effective in improving students' revisions, but benefits were also noted on subsequent first drafts (Hillocks, 1986).

Thematic Development. *Elaborating Ideas.* The "star strategy" (see Figure 5.3) can be used to organize ideas and elaborate on details.

- Write topic/main idea as reminder to help stay on track.

- List related ideas inside each point of star (not all elements will be used every time).

- Number each aspect (1. who?, 2. where?, etc.) in the order to be presented as a paragraph.

Syntactic Development.   Students combine sentences and build sentences from phrases, creating more complex sentences from simpler ones. Various strategies for the manipulation of syntax are taught, including use of modifiers, connectives, and embedding.

Revision Techniques.   Students who do not have the benefit of word processors may be reluctant to revise if they dread having to recopy their entire efforts. Many different revision techniques can be taught to students, including the following:

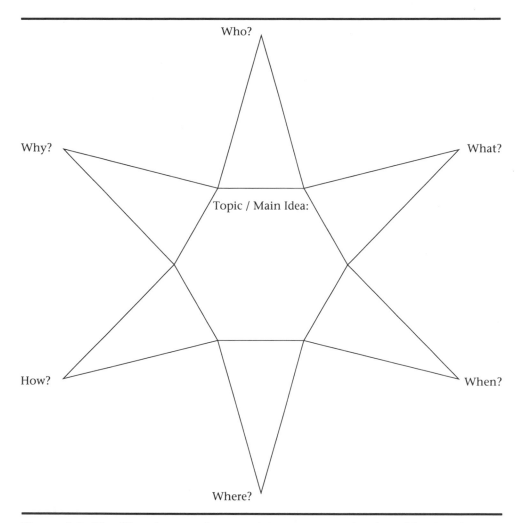

Figure 5.3. The "Star Strategy," a prewriting organizer developed by S. Taber, Institute for Learning and Development.

- Write drafts double-spaced by skipping every other line to accommodate revisions.

- Cross out: *Yes,* it is OK to cross out text that is being revised. It is better than erasing, as the writer can still see the original text.

- Insert small pieces of new text using carets to indicate position.

- Insert larger pieces of new text with a numbering system or "spider legs" (e.g., strips of paper with the new text are taped into the proper location).

- Reorganize using cut and paste.

Teach Self-Checking and Editing Strategies

Editing Checklists.   Develop procedure checklists with students depending on need. Acronyms are often helpful—for example, COPS, which focuses students on capitalization, overall appearance, end punctuation, and spelling (Deshler & Schumaker, 1986).

- In the primary grades, COPS may be modified as Capitals, Order, Periods, Spelling.
- In the middle grades, COPS can incorporate the skills needed from each student's perspective:

  C = Capitalization

  O = Organization/overall appearance

  P = Punctuation

  S = Spelling/sentence structure

- An alternate acronym for the middle grades is STOPS (developed by Colin Meltzer, a sixth-grade student).

  S = Sentence structure

  T = Tenses

  O = Organization/order

  P = Punctuation

  S = Spelling

  This is helpful for students who confuse verb forms and tenses.

- In high school, use "C. SCOOPS" (developed by Susan Taber, Educational Specialist, Institute for Learning and Development, Chelmsford, MA).

  C = Content

  S = Sentence structure

  C = Capitalization

  O = Organization

  O = Order and neatness

  P = Punctuation

  S = Spelling

Self-Monitoring.   Develop students' awareness of errors.

- Students circle words they know to be misspelled, underline those that may be misspelled.

- Students mark suspected punctuation errors with a red pencil and attempt correction.

- Teacher rewards *awareness* in the same manner as he or she rewards *correctness*.

Proofreading Paragraphs.   Guide students through the proofreading process.

- **Problem:** Repetition of same word several times
  Solution: 1. Use Franklin Wordmaster or thesaurus to find synonyms.
  2. Rearrange sentence to eliminate word.

- **Problem:** Inconsistent verb tense
  Solution: 1. Decide on which tense to write in (past, present, future).
  2. Review writing and change tenses to stay consistent.

- **Problem:** Run-on sentences
  Solution: 1. Break down wordy sentences (eliminate *and*).
  2. Add signal words where appropriate (*however, first of all, finally, in other words,* etc.).
  3. Use semicolons to break up sentences, if appropriate.
  4. Remember the run-on rule: If you have to take a breath or two while reading the sentence aloud, it's a run-on (Susan Taber, Institute for Learning and Development).

Use of Word Processors and Spell-Checkers

Using word processors allows students to focus on the ideas they are attempting to express. This reduces the demands on fine-motor skills, letter formation, and spatial organization that often impede the progress of students with learning difficulties. Students who use word processors may also be more apt to revise their writing, because they do not have to rewrite or "mess up" their papers. Students with learning difficulties need opportunities to revise easily in order to bypass their problems with handwriting and spelling. However, they will need opportunities to write with a pencil so that they can practice and become more proficient.

- Many appropriate software programs are available that are easy to learn (e.g., Bank Street Writer, the Writing Center).

- Keyboarding skills can also be taught using appropriate software (e.g., Type to Learn by Sunburst).

How Can You Help Students Become Better Writers?

You can use several methods to help your students improve their writing skills, including the following:

How To Help Your Students Become Better Writers

❑ Provide constant practice and spiraling.

❑ Help students internalize strategies so these can be used spontaneously.

❑ Insure that students understand the importance of the different stages of writing.

❑ Success helps students value the strategies and use them independently in many different contexts and settings.

❑ Remember that students with learning difficulties need much more review, practice, repetition, and success than their peers in order to use these strategies independently. They need to learn to believe in themselves as writers and to recognize their strengths while learning to overcome the impact of their weaknesses.

© 1996 PRO-ED, Inc.

How might you use these strategies during a writing lesson? Remember Sara, Bill, and Tom from the reading lesson in Chapter 4 (see Table 4.2)? Now imagine that it is 6 years later and they are in your 10th-grade English or social studies class. You have just completed the autobiography of a famous person, and you would like students in your class to write their own autobiographies. The class consists of 25 students in a heterogeneous grouping. Table 5.2 describes the skills of our three students.

Table 5.2. Writing Skills of Individual Students

Sara	Bill	Tom
LD; processing skills are strong in visual channel, weak in language; uses concrete language and sentences when writing	LD; strong oral language, good comprehension, poor phonological awareness; good ideas for writing but poor fluency, poor spelling and handwriting, limited productivity	ADD; overfocuses on details, disorganized, poor self-monitoring

© 1996 PRO-ED, Inc.

Set Goals for the Paper

Purpose.   Discuss with students the purpose of the assignment. Students are expected to write an autobiography in which they project their lives into the future. Each student must describe the accomplishments or contributions he or she has made. Students are expected to write about authentic experiences in their childhoods that helped shape the type of people they have become.

Structure of the Paper.   In the planning stages, students must first fantasize about the future before they can determine which childhood experiences are relevant. However, the paper will be written chronologically, starting with their childhood. The structure will be similar to the structure used in the autobiography they have finished reading.

Sources of Information.   Brainstorm with students regarding where they can find information. Sources could include personal experiences; interviews with family members; photo albums or scrapbooks; research in the person's chosen field of expertise. Also, mention that the class will be participating in activities to help all students secure ideas.

Expectations Regarding Writing Skills.   Students should focus their first drafts on organization, creativity, and thematic continuity. Expectations for sentence structure, spelling, and mechanics will be individualized based on students' abilities and editing checklists.

Time Lines.   Provide calendars with due dates at various points in time. Develop study plans with students to help them achieve these goals. These plans can be individualized, and students with more significant organizational difficulties can be monitored more frequently than those with strengths in this area. Table 5.3 shows accommodations to address the individual learning styles of our three students.

Table 5.3. Accommodations for Individual Learning Styles

Sara	Bill	Tom
Expected to use correct spelling and mechanics; sentence combining activities will be used to enhance grammatical complexity	Expected to use complex sentence structures with rich vocabulary and language usage; will use a word processor and spell-check feature, but drafts will not be checked for spelling; expected to use capitalization and ending punctuation only	Will develop a study plan with the teacher and set daily goals for the assignment and strategies for attaining these goals; will be responsible for all skills on his editing checklist

Secure Ideas

- Use *guided imagery* and a modification of the mining for topics activity in Appendix 4 to help students develop creative ideas. This is particularly helpful for students with strong visual skills who have weaknesses in word retrieval or language processing. Have students close their eyes, with pencil and paper handy. Conduct a guided imagery activity similar to the one described below:

> Imagine yourself 20 years from now. You wake up and dress for another busy day. What are you wearing? A suit and tie? a dress? a uniform? casual clothes? Picture it in your mind. You walk into the kitchen and can smell the coffee brewing. You pour yourself a cup of coffee as you reach for the morning paper. In the newspaper there is an article about yourself. In what section of the paper is it? front page? business? health? arts and entertainment? learning? sports? What have you done that has made you famous? Perhaps you have made a large contribution to the field you have chosen as a career. Maybe you have completed notable volunteer work for a charitable cause, or for a community, or for a religious organization. Maybe you have been recognized for an athletic achievement. Along with the article is an accompanying photograph. What are you doing? Who is with you? What does the caption say? Now, with your eyes closed, review the scenario you have just imagined, starting with getting dressed in the morning. After you have finished, record the description on your paper.

- Brainstorm childhood experiences that have shaped your future interests and that are related to the achievements you have imagined.

- Secure additional ideas using the methods discussed above (e.g., interviews).

Accommodations for the three example students are shown in Table 5.4.

Organize Ideas

- *Text Structure:* Use the autobiography of the famous person that preceded this lesson as a model to develop an understanding of the chronological text structure from a writer's point of view. How did the author determine which experiences were relevant? Which periods in his life received the most attention? Why? Also, discuss which general

Table 5.4. Accommodations for Guided Imagery

Sara	Bill	Tom
During the guided imagery activity, speak slowly to accommodate her processing rate. After the activity, have her sketch her image before writing it.	Have him tape-record his interviews instead of writing them. This will reduce the fine-motor demands of writing.	After the brainstorming activity, help him to identify specific childhood experiences that are relevant and provide the necessary structure. Provide preferential seating during guided imagery.

information should be included in each autobiography (e.g., birth date, place, family makeup, moves, development of roles of significant family members).

- *Semantic Mapping:* Organize ideas in a sequential fashion from the above discussion. Then have students use the same type of map to record the ideas for their own autobiographies.

Accommodations for the three students for this activity are shown in Table 5.5.

Model Strategies to Encourage Self-Regulation

Model strategies for prioritizing information by completing a semantic map with the class that sequences ideas for your own autobiography. For example, describe various childhood experiences you have had. Discuss with students which of these experiences may have led to interest in pursuing a career in education. Prioritize these ideas with students, including your "self-talk" in determining which ideas to include and which to delete.

Table 5.5. Accommodations to Help Students Organize Ideas

Sara	Bill	Tom
Use a *"wh- question list"* (i.e., *who, what, when, where, why, how*) to help her retrieve additional information to add to the map.	Have him draw lines on his map to assist his word alignment.	Structure this activity further by creating headings for each part of the map. This will help him to focus his ideas. Use *wh*-questions as with Sara.

Revise for Organization, Creativity, and Thematic Continuity

- Help students revise their drafts and plan future directions through teacher and peer conferences. Students with difficulties in organization and prioritizing may need additional conference time. These can be scheduled into the projected time lines.

- Teach revision techniques.

- Students could use a word processor to minimize the fine-motor and organizational demands of writing.

Accommodations for Sam, Bill, and Tom are shown in Table 5.6.

Revise for Sentence Structure, Spelling, and Mechanics

- Use sentence combining with examples from students' writing to help them develop complex sentence structures.

- Teach students one or two more editing skills based on individual needs and include an editing checklist.
- Have students use their editing checklists to edit their papers.

Accommodations for the three students are shown in Table 5.7.

Table 5.6. Accommodations to Help Students with Revision and Organization of Ideas

Sara	Bill	Tom
Have her circle frequently used words or concrete vocabulary and change these using a thesaurus.	Schedule additional conferences to help him revise for clarity and elaborate on his ideas (to increase productivity).	Schedule additional conferences to assist his development of topic sentences and his transitions between paragraphs.

© 1996 PRO-ED, Inc.

Table 5.7. Accommodations to Help Students with Editing for Sentence Structure, Spelling, and Mechanics

Sara	Bill	Tom
Help her develop complex sentences through sentence combining and sentence-building activities.	Have him circle words he thinks are misspelled and attempt to correct these. Use the spell-checker feature on the word processor and compare number of errors.	Have him read his paper out loud during the editing process. Have him use his editing checklist and look for one error pattern at a time (e.g., COPS).

© 1996 PRO-ED, Inc.

Chapter 6

Automaticity and Problem Solving in Mathematics

Bethany Roditi

Why Teach Strategies in Mathematics?

An increased emphasis has been placed in math classrooms on speed and organization since the nationwide math curriculum shift from rote computation skills to meaningful problem solving. Students are now required to learn multiple strategies for solving math problems, whether or not they have automatized basic arithmetic facts or quantitative concepts and procedures. However, to estimate and to solve math problems, students need to recall math facts accurately and rapidly. In addition, they are expected to decide which tool is best to use in the process of solving math problems: mental computation, calculators, computers, software, or pencil and paper. Further, students have to plan, to formulate, and to use effective problem-solving strategies.

For students with difficulties in memorizing math facts, the emphasis on logical reasoning and problem solving is a welcome relief. However, they may be overwhelmed with the many problem-solving strategies that they are expected to learn. Students with organizational problems and impulsivity need structure, routines, and clear-cut systems for solving specific problems. Mathematics instruction must be designed to provide a balance between rote learning and meaningful problem solving. To accomplish this in a heterogeneous classroom where students have multiple learning profiles, math skills as well as math strategies must be taught explicitly. Further, all students, especially those with learning problems, need to learn which strategies work best for them and when to apply these strategies. The question, then, is how can you teach students to be strategic math problem-solvers in the context of today's classroom, with limited time and resources available?

Can Students Be Taught to Be Strategic Problem-Solvers?

Although you cannot change your students' basic learning styles, you do have the ability to influence their problem-solving approaches. Here are some general principles to guide your teaching strategies in the classroom:

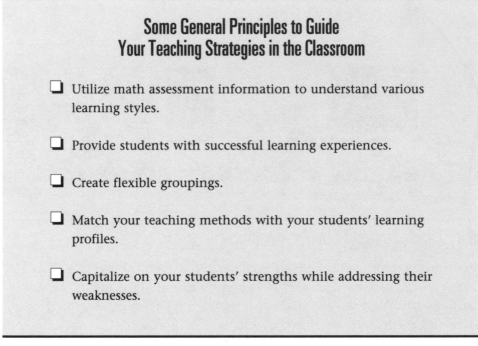

Some General Principles to Guide Your Teaching Strategies in the Classroom

❏ Utilize math assessment information to understand various learning styles.

❏ Provide students with successful learning experiences.

❏ Create flexible groupings.

❏ Match your teaching methods with your students' learning profiles.

❏ Capitalize on your students' strengths while addressing their weaknesses.

© 1996 PRO-ED, Inc.

By matching students' learning styles with specific strategies and teaching methods, you give students opportunities to succeed in math. You build their self-confidence so they perceive themselves as capable math problem-solvers for the first time. Ask yourself questions such as these:

- Which students will benefit from practicing a draw-it-out strategy as opposed to an organized list strategy?

- Which students will need more time to practice their multiplication facts?

- Which students will benefit from enrichment projects or curriculum extensions?

Thus, *you* can be strategic—that is, you can decide what teaching methods and materials to use and how to use these most effectively in a classroom where students have multiple learning profiles.

Can Traditional Math Assessment Help?

Math assessment frequently confirms what you already know about your students from observing them in class. The results often pinpoint specific gaps in your students' knowledge of quantitative concepts and skills (i.e., addition/subtraction, multiplication/division, fractions, decimals, percent, time, measurement, and geometry). Typically, test results are based on the accuracy of your students' answers and yield a grade-score equivalent. Table 6.1 is a list of currently used math tests and subtests.

Traditional, subject-centered forms of math assessment such as those listed in Table 6.1 are effective in identifying what math skills to teach. However, you must also be aware of your students' cognitive and learning profiles to know how to teach them.

Table 6.1. Currently Used Math Tests

Math Tests and Subtests	Grade Range
Brigance Diagnostic Comprehensive Inventory of Basic Skills	K–9
Brigance Diagnostic Inventory of Essential Skills	4–12
California Achievement Tests	K–12
Diagnostic Mathematics Inventory/Mathematics Systems	1–12
Diagnostic Tests and Self-Helps in Arithmetic	3–8
Enright Diagnostic Inventory of Basic Arithmetic Skills	
Iowa Tests of Basic Skills	P–3
Kaufman Tests of Educational Achievement	1–12
Key Math–Revised	K–6
Metropolitan Achievement Tests	
Peabody Individual Achievement Test–Revised	K–12
Sequential Assessment of Mathematics Inventories (SAMI)	K–8
Test of Computational Processes	
Stanford Diagnostic Mathematics Test	K–12
Surveys of Problem-Solving and Educational Skills (SPES)	4–9
Test of Mathematics Ability (TOMA)	3–12
Wechsler Individual Achievement Test	
Wechsler Individual Intelligence Tests III–R—Arithmetic Subtest	
Wide Range Achievement Test–R (WRAT-R)	K–12
Woodcock-Johnson Psychoeducational Battery/Achievement–R	P–12
Woodcock-Johnson Psychoeducational Battery	3–Adult
Tests of Cognitive Ability	

Note. From "Mathematics Assessment and Strategy Instruction" by B. Roditi in *Strategy Assessment and Instruction for Students with Learning Disabilities: From Theory to Practice* by L. Meltzer (Ed.), 1993, Austin, Texas: PRO-ED.

What Cognitive and Learning Processes Are Relevant?

Students with learning difficulties from elementary to high school often experience difficulties in one or more areas. Underlying cognitive, linguistic, and social-emotional processes may affect your students' ability to learn math. The following checklist may help you document your observations and test results:

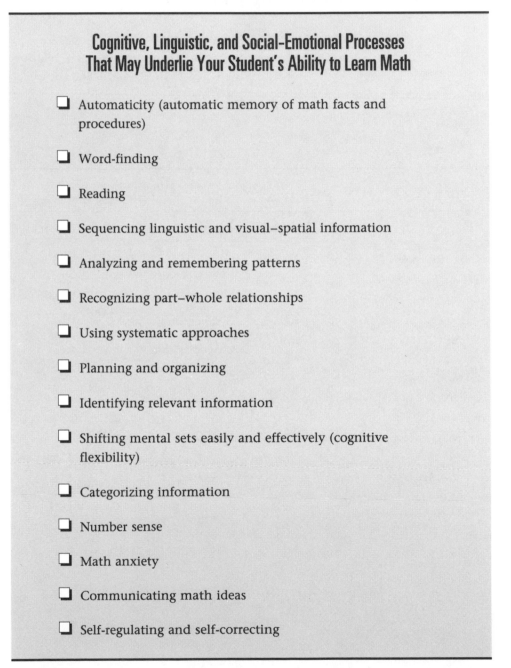

Cognitive, Linguistic, and Social-Emotional Processes That May Underlie Your Student's Ability to Learn Math

❑ Automaticity (automatic memory of math facts and procedures)

❑ Word-finding

❑ Reading

❑ Sequencing linguistic and visual–spatial information

❑ Analyzing and remembering patterns

❑ Recognizing part–whole relationships

❑ Using systematic approaches

❑ Planning and organizing

❑ Identifying relevant information

❑ Shifting mental sets easily and effectively (cognitive flexibility)

❑ Categorizing information

❑ Number sense

❑ Math anxiety

❑ Communicating math ideas

❑ Self-regulating and self-correcting

In each of these areas, teachers need to be aware of the variations in strengths and weaknesses that characterize each student. This will help target direct math strategy instruction and create effective, flexible groupings in the math classroom.

How Do Cognitive and Language Skills Affect Math Learning?

To Determine Which Cognitive Strategies to Assess, Ask Yourself: Is My Student . . .

❏ using systematic approaches?

❏ identifying relevant information?

❏ shifting easily from one approach to another?

❏ analyzing patterns?

❏ recognizing part–whole relationships?

❏ self-monitoring and self-correcting?

Although it is important to identify your students' prior math knowledge, it is also critical to be aware of the cognitive and language strategies that affect math learning in your class. Most math tests are not designed to examine how efficiently students use cognitive strategies to solve math problems. You can gather this information by observing your students while they are working independently, in small groups, and with the entire class.

Many students with learning problems, especially those who also have attentional problems, often use random and impulsive approaches when solving math problems. When presented with a word problem, for example, they quickly call out, "I have to add, no . . . multiply . . . no, subtract . . . divide?" They often guess without a clear picture of the major question. These students benefit from learning organizational strategies that help them think through the problem and plan and predict before they attempt to calculate and solve. Specific strategies (e.g., how to develop and use advanced graphic organizers) are described in the section titled "The Math Problem-Solving Process" later in this chapter. These strategies also help students who confuse important information with extra, irrelevant information. You can encourage your students to think flexibly by helping them identify different ways to solve the same problem. Students can also learn how to use different strategies for various types of problems. For those students who have difficulty seeing part–whole relationships and analyzing patterns, you can demonstrate how particular patterns develop (e.g., Terrific Tens, discussed later in this chapter) so that they can begin to identify these patterns on their own.

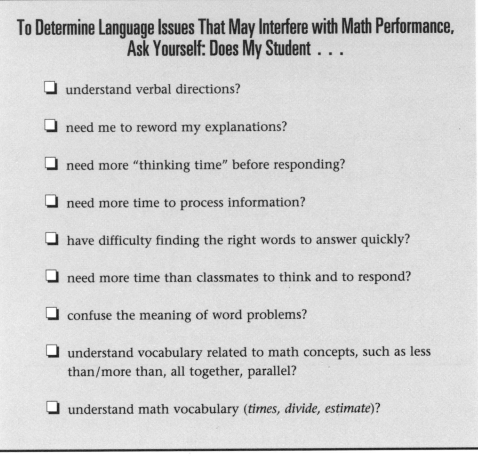

To Determine Language Issues That May Interfere with Math Performance, Ask Yourself: Does My Student . . .

❏ understand verbal directions?

❏ need me to reword my explanations?

❏ need more "thinking time" before responding?

❏ need more time to process information?

❏ have difficulty finding the right words to answer quickly?

❏ need more time than classmates to think and to respond?

❏ confuse the meaning of word problems?

❏ understand vocabulary related to math concepts, such as less than/more than, all together, parallel?

❏ understand math vocabulary (*times, divide, estimate*)?

Do Your Students Have an Intuitive Number Sense?

Number sense refers to the ability to understand quantitative concepts and number meanings. At the number level, some of your students look at the digit symbol 7 and automatically attach meaning to it, whereas other students look at the same digit 7 and think they are reading a foreign language. While performing paper-and-pencil calculations in the process of solving a math word problem, your students are expected to associate quantitative concepts with specific operational symbols (e.g., + means addition). At the application level, students must rely on their number sense to make sure the problem-solving process and solution make sense.

To help your students understand quantitative concepts and symbols, see the list in Table 6.2.

Students with learning problems in the math area often exhibit cognitive strategy deficits, and some lack an intuitive number sense. These deficits interfere with their math performance in many ways. Math assessment should help you differentiate students who do not have a strong number sense and determine under what conditions numbers become meaningful.

•••

What Areas Should You Target?

Math skills and examples of the use of those skills are shown in Table 6.3.

Strategies to Insure Automatic Memorization of Math Facts

Timed tests on math facts and complex computations pose problems for many students with learning difficulties. They often show weaknesses in their automatic memory for math facts, resulting in slow, effortful, and often inaccurate calculations. By identifying these students, you can provide them with direct strategic math instruction to tackle this particular problem at an early stage. By doing so,

---

Table 6.2. How to Help Your Students Understand Quantitative Concepts and Symbols

To assess number sense:

- Observe your students while they engage in various math activities.
- Use multisensory formats.
- Use dialogue to check your students' understanding of quantitative concepts and symbols.
- Examine number sense at multiple levels of processing:

  Number Level

  - Digit meaning (7)
  - Number word meaning (seven)
  - Number word meaning in context (seven cars)

  Algorithm Level

  - Operation symbol meaning ($+ - \times$)
  - Rules or procedures (long division procedure—numbers alone)
  - Rules or procedures in context of a meaningful problem

  Application Level (Problem Solving)

  - Effective selection and use of cognitive strategies
  - Checking reasonableness of partial and final solutions

Ask yourself:

- Should number symbols be paired with graphic representations?
- Does the use of concrete aids enhance number meaning?
- Should all numbers be presented in a meaningful context?

Table 6.3. Math Strategy Instruction

Goals	Examples
Automaticity	Automatic memory for math facts
Number sense	Understanding time and money
Problem solving	Solving word problems

you can prevent them from experiencing years of frustration and failure in math. For years, worksheet practice, timed drill tests, and flash cards were the prescribed teaching methods used for building math fact recall. However, there are always some students who cannot master their math facts. Fortunately, new research-based techniques and computer technology currently offer teaching methods that do help these students who have found it next to impossible to automatize their math facts.

Until recently, you most likely relied on drill-and-practice activities using flash cards, fact table exercises, and worksheets to help your students memorize the basic math facts. Despite this reinforcement, many students with learning difficulties need a more systematic, strategic approach to build speed and accuracy for recalling math facts. Hasselbring, Goin, and Bradford (1988) provided a systematic, research-based technique for helping students with learning difficulties learn how to automatize math facts. Here are some important principles and guidelines to follow:

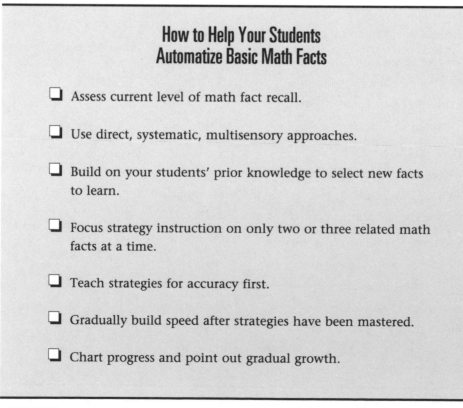

How to Help Your Students Automatize Basic Math Facts

❏ Assess current level of math fact recall.

❏ Use direct, systematic, multisensory approaches.

❏ Build on your students' prior knowledge to select new facts to learn.

❏ Focus strategy instruction on only two or three related math facts at a time.

❏ Teach strategies for accuracy first.

❏ Gradually build speed after strategies have been mastered.

❏ Chart progress and point out gradual growth.

1. **Assess current level of automaticity (math fact recall).** From observations of students' work in math class, you may be able to identify some, but not all, students who have or have not automatized their math facts. Some students develop their own idiosyncratic strategies for figuring out math facts that they have not automatized, but this extra mental work soon becomes inefficient. As problem-solving demands increase, they can no longer divert their attention to figure out a fact and refocus their attention on the problem at hand. Math assessment can identify those students who compensate for a lack of automaticity and can pinpoint those specific math facts that are problematic.

2. **Use a direct, systematic, multisensory approach.** By using a systematic approach to assess the automatic recall of math facts, you can differentiate math facts into three distinct groups:

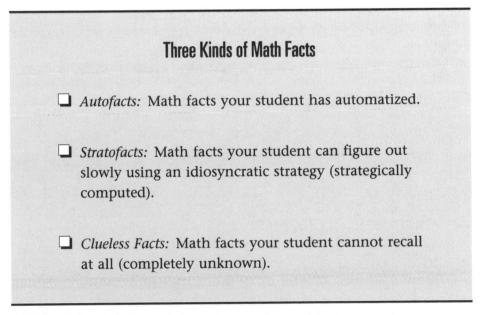

Three Kinds of Math Facts

❏ *Autofacts:* Math facts your student has automatized.

❏ *Stratofacts:* Math facts your student can figure out slowly using an idiosyncratic strategy (strategically computed).

❏ *Clueless Facts:* Math facts your student cannot recall at all (completely unknown).

© 1996 PRO-ED, Inc.

Math fact table grids, either teacher-made or purchased, are excellent visual aids for documentation (see example in Figure 6.1). By analyzing automatic memory of facts, you help your students realize that memorizing math facts can be simplified. When the number of facts to learn is reduced, the task becomes less overwhelming and less of a working memory load.

3. **Build on students' prior knowledge.** To build on students' prior knowledge, ask yourself:

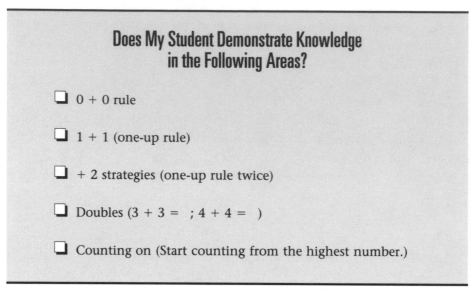

Does My Student Demonstrate Knowledge in the Following Areas?

❑ 0 + 0 rule

❑ 1 + 1 (one-up rule)

❑ + 2 strategies (one-up rule twice)

❑ Doubles (3 + 3 = ; 4 + 4 =)

❑ Counting on (Start counting from the highest number.)

1 Rule (Add-on-One Rule or Incrementing Rule): Many students enjoy "naming" the rule themselves. Active involvement often increases their chances of remembering and applying the rule later. Most elementary students can easily apply this rule. They soon realize that they now "own" 20 more facts on the 100-space math fact grid, thus motivating them to automatize more facts.

	0	1	2	3	4	5	6	7	8	9
0										
1										
2										
3										
4										
5										
6										
7										
8										
9										

A- AUTOFACT   S- STRATOFACT   U- UNKNOWN FACT

Figure 6.1. A math fact table grid.

Up-One Rule (+1)

Reciprocals

1 + 1 = ...2	1 + 1 = 2
2 + 1 = ...3	1 + 2 = 3
3 + 1 = ...4	1 + 3 = 4
4 + 1 = ...5	1 + 4 = 5
150 + 1 = 151	1 + 150 = 151
151 + 1 = 152	1 + 151 = 152	Can you create more examples?

Doubles Rule

1 + 1 = 2
2 + 2 = 4
3 + 3 = 6
4 + 4 = 8
5 + 5 = 10
6 + 6 = 12

Students tend to easily remember these facts. They enjoy accumulating 10 more facts, thus adding to their repertoire of stratofacts.

+2 Strategies

- Use the Up-One 1 rule twice. Some students quickly learn to use their prior knowledge of the +1 rule and use the rule twice in a row. They find an autofact, like 6 + 0 = 6, then they can produce 6 + 1 = 7, then 6 + 2 = 8 by mentally incrementing twice.

- Use a visual, counting-up approach.
  0 + 5 = 5
  5 + 0 = 5 (Count up twice from the larger number.)
  5 + 1 = 5 ***** + * = 6
  5 + 2 = ***** + ** = 7

4. **Focus strategy instruction on only two or three related facts.** Encourage your students to develop strategies that capitalize on their strengths and interests. Math rings, which emphasize mastered facts rather than "facts to learn" and strategies for remembering rather than just the right answers, can be very rewarding and can provide an incentive to add on more and more facts (see Figure 6.2). Students with learning difficulties often require continual practice in reviewing newly automatized facts to store these facts in their long-term memory. Math rings can be placed on the students' mirrors or in another convenient place as a reminder to review these on a daily basis. Some teachers ask their students to place their rings inside their math strategy notebooks for use during practice lab or "strategy time." These classroom management techniques are described in more detail later in this chapter.

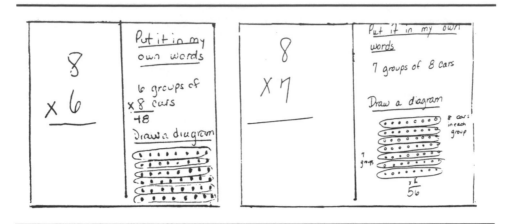

Figure 6.2. An example of a math ring.

5. **Teach strategies for accuracy before building speed.**

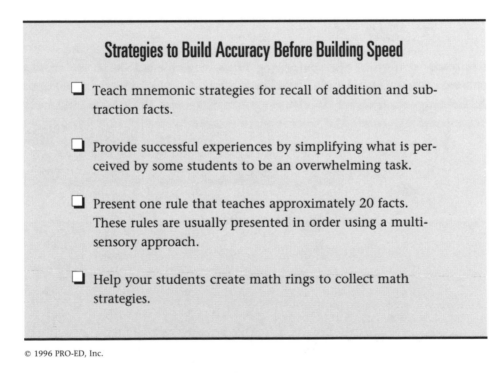

Strategies to Build Accuracy Before Building Speed

☐ Teach mnemonic strategies for recall of addition and subtraction facts.

☐ Provide successful experiences by simplifying what is perceived by some students to be an overwhelming task.

☐ Present one rule that teaches approximately 20 facts. These rules are usually presented in order using a multisensory approach.

☐ Help your students create math rings to collect math strategies.

6. **"Talk" mathematics in a thoughtfully sequenced way.**

  • Use dialogue that begins at a point of prior knowledge.

  • Teach rules directly.

  • Give many examples.

  • Set up question-answer sequences so that they lead to successful responses.

7. **Summarize rules verbally and visually.**

- Remember to use a multisensory approach.

- Have your students repeat rules in their own words (oral).

- Draw a rule box on the chalkboard (visual).

- Give students time to write the rule in their math strategy notebooks with one example.

- Model on the board or on the overhead how students can summarize rules by making summary boxes or strategy clouds in their strategy notebooks (see Figure 6.3).

8. **Teach three-column note-taking strategy to link symbolic representations of numbers with graphic representations** (see Figure 6.4).

9. **Ask students to write out number families.** Number families are clusters of related math facts, including addition and subtraction (or multiplication and division) and their reciprocals. For example:

$$1+9=10 \qquad 9+1=10 \qquad 10-1=9 \qquad 10-9=1 \text{ (written vertically)}$$

You can ask your students to represent these number sentences in various ways. Some students could draw objects representing these number sentences. Students who have difficulty drawing could use math manipulatives. You are helping all students to understand that addition and subtraction are interrelated concepts, not discrete operations. Further, you are helping students with memory weaknesses. By clustering numbers in this way, your students only have to retrieve one family of math facts that unleashes the others rather than remembering 100 separate math facts. By using a multisensory approach during this

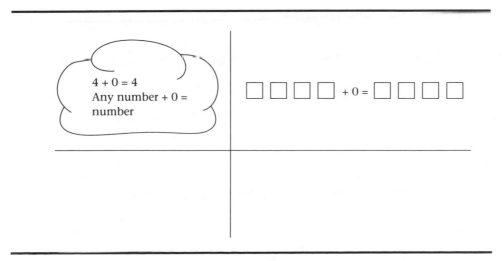

Figure 6.3. Summary boxes or strategy clouds for summarizing math rules.

process whereby the students "talk" and "hear" math facts, picture them, and write about them, you can rest assured that you are addressing the multiple learning styles in your classroom (see Figure 6.5).

10. Develop number patterns together.

Problem or vocabulary word	Golden rule	Example

Figure 6.4. A sample three-column form to summarize math rules.

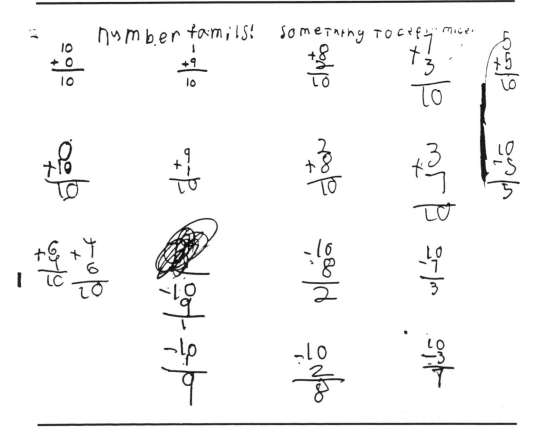

Figure 6.5. Number families: A strategy for learning clusters of related addition and subtraction facts.

11. **Teach the "Terrific Tens" strategy directly.** Some students with learning difficulties do not recognize patterns, but if you develop a pattern with them as in the example shown in Figure 6.6, they soon realize that as they increase one number on top, they are decreasing a number on the bottom. They can visualize the reciprocals. Those students who cannot easily remember the math facts by rote quickly learn that they can generate 10 facts from one fact. If they know that $1+9=10$, they can figure the rest of the pattern out themselves.

12. **Practice using strategies, but no time pressures yet!**

13. **Create card games.** Students with learning difficulties need more reinforcement and spiral teaching than the average student. Drill and practice can be effective if implemented within a card game context. The advantage of using cards is the pairing of both the number symbols and graphic representations simultaneously, thereby enhancing number sense while, at the same time, building automaticity (see Figure 6.7). Fraction cards are also available that pair the fraction with a visual drawing that represents the same fraction.

14. **Teach the "TEEN" Strategy.**
    $10+3=$thir TEEN $= 13$; $10+5=$fif TEEN $= 15$; $10+7=$seven TEEN $=$ 17
    $10+4=$four TEEN $= 14$; $10+6=$six TEEN $= 16$; $10+8=$eight TEEN $=$ 18

$$10 + 0 = 10$$
$$10 + 1 = 11$$
$$10 + 2 = 12$$
$$10 + 3 = 13$$
$$10 + 4 = 14$$
$$10 + 5 = 15$$
$$10 + 6 = 16$$
$$10 + 7 = 17$$
$$10 + 8 = 18$$
$$10 + 9 = 19$$

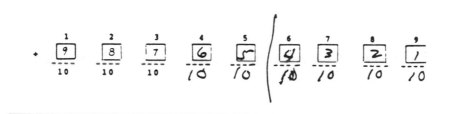

Figure 6.6. The "Terrific Tens" strategy.

Figure 6.7. Example of "Terrific Tens" strategy for memorization of math facts.

By using both the sound of your voice to emphasize the TEEN and the visual printed word TEEN, you can help those students who need visual or auditory cues to remember the facts and their reciprocals.

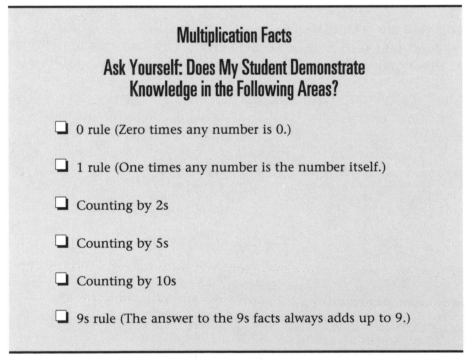

Multiplication Facts

Ask Yourself: Does My Student Demonstrate Knowledge in the Following Areas?

❏ 0 rule (Zero times any number is 0.)

❏ 1 rule (One times any number is the number itself.)

❏ Counting by 2s

❏ Counting by 5s

❏ Counting by 10s

❏ 9s rule (The answer to the 9s facts always adds up to 9.)

Use direct, systematic, multisensory instruction for learning multiplication facts.

15. **Teach the "9s Rule."** Students are fascinated when they learn the "magical" 9s rule of multiplication. They can use their prior knowledge of all the numbers that add up to 9 (e.g., 4+5, 3+6, 2+7, and 1+8). They can also use a count-backwards strategy to find the first number. This strategy, together with students' prior knowledge of easier 9s facts, helps them recall the 9s facts quickly. An example on a math ring card is shown in Figure 6.8.

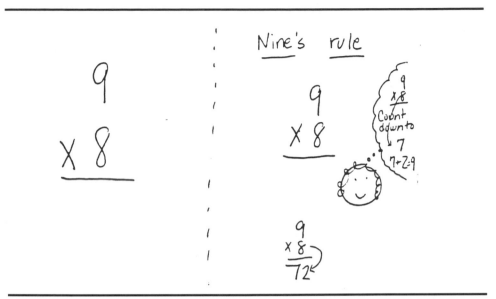

Figure 6.8. An example of use of the 9s rule.

16. **Identify a pattern of strategies that emerge and create a checklist with your students to figure out difficult facts.**

  • 0 rule

  • 1 rule

  • 2s rule

  • Does the number end in a 5 or a 10?

  • 9s rule

  • Count backwards?

  • Count backwards by 2s?

Other examples of multiplication strategies are listed below.

17. **Teach a count-backwards strategy for 8 × 7 = 56** (see Figure 6.9).

18. **Teach a count-backwards-by-2s strategy for 6 × 4 = 24 or 7 × 6 = 42** (see Figure 6.10).

19. **Teach strategies in combination with prior knowledge of a mastered fact.** For example, if your students know that 7 × 5 = 35, they know that the next group of 7s will be in the 40s (7 × 6 =).

20. **Build speed gradually.** *Beat the Snap Game:* As your students enter your classroom, give them a math fact to recall (one of their new facts). You can time them by holding your hand up high and gradually letting it fall as you count out seconds. You can snap your fingers at the 5-second count to see if your students can recall the fact that quickly. Then, you can reduce the number of

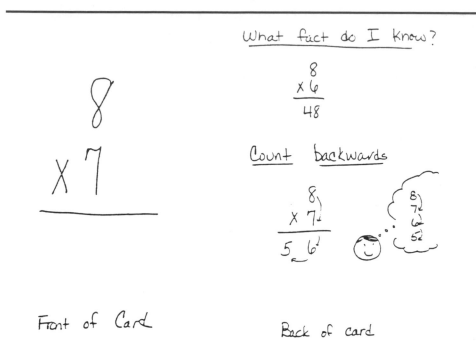

Figure 6.9. A count backwards strategy for 8 × 7 = 56.

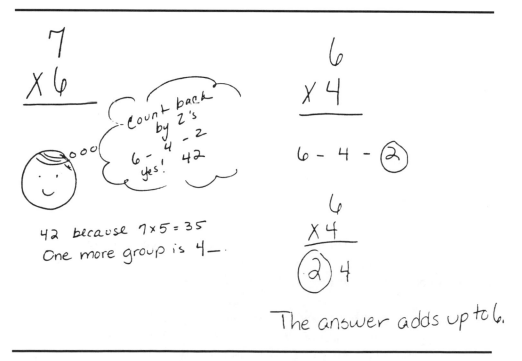

Figure 6.10. A count backwards by 2s strategy for 6 × 4 = 24 or 7 × 6 = 42.

seconds before you snap your fingers to show your students that they are recalling the facts more quickly. Their time may improve from 5 seconds to 1 second, and then they become automatic in their recall over just a day or 2.

21. **Use "shell" software programs.** To enhance automaticity further, you can provide your students with an opportunity to practice just the autofacts and two new stratofacts without confusing the situation with "clueless" facts. Shell software programs allow you or your students to program just those math facts under consideration into the computer-based activity. The aim is to gradually increase the repertoire of stratofacts to the point that timed practices may begin.

22. **Teach strategies first, then gradually build speed.** It is very important to note that no fact should be drilled under timed conditions until the strategy is learned and the math fact is recalled with ease. In addition, shell programs (e.g., Robomath by Mindplay) allow students to bypass their handwriting and/or visual-spatial difficulties. They can focus on math rather than on their writing or on lining up numbers on a page. By using shell software in a systematic way, students can improve the automatic math fact recall within a learning environment that is enjoyable and success oriented.

23. **Set up practice labs in your classroom (structured opportunities for guided practice).** Set aside time (5 to 15 minutes) during the day for all your students to practice a particular skill or strategy. During these practice labs, you can individualize or group students so that they can work on their own instructional goals. By using math strategy notebooks and flexible groups, these practice labs can be effective for the slow learner, the gifted student who needs time for curriculum extension, those students who need more time to process information and to complete their work, and those students who simply need time to practice.

24. **Minimize the teaching of pencil-and-paper computation; instead, encourage the use of calculators for computation.** The National Council of Teachers of Mathematics's (NCTM) New Standards of Mathematics Education emphasizes that *all* students should have access to calculators at all times. If your curriculum continues to emphasize paper-and-pencil calculations, you can minimize the amount of teaching time spent on this soon-to-be-obsolete skill in our technological society. At least, allow your students to check their answers with the calculator. Some students may prefer to use a calculator with a printout to efficiently check for accuracy. Others, who have memory and organizational difficulties, may need to write down each numerical entry before entering the numbers into the calculator.

The Math Problem-Solving Process

Teach math problem-solving strategically. First, you can review the math problem-solving process and analyze where your students may be encountering initial difficulty (see Table 6.4). Most students with learning difficulties experience significant difficulty at the transfer phase and the organization phase. Once you are aware of the breakdown, there are a number of strategies that you can teach your students to overcome this problem. Some of the strategies include the following:

1. **Teach students using multisensory techniques such as the CSA method** (Miller & Mercer, 1993). You can balance your presentation style by incorporating verbal explanation and discussion with visual models and hands-on learning experiences. The CSA method is a research-based teaching method that embodies multisensory instruction in a structured and systematic way (see Table 6.5).

    Some students cannot conceptualize quantitative concepts unless they are presented first in a concrete manner within a meaningful context. By using the CSA technique, you can insure that all of your students' learning styles are considered. For example, students who have language difficulties can benefit from the pictures and hands-on manipulatives. Students who have visual-spatial difficulties can rely on verbal explanations and discussions that combine visual models with hands-on learning. In some manipulative programs, the

Table 6.4. Mathematical Problem-Solving Process

Goals	Ask yourself: Can my student . . .
Reading	read the problem independently?
Orientation	conceptualize the problem?
Transfer	translate the problem from one representation to another (shift sets among words, pictures, objects, tables, graphs)?
Organization	plan a path to the solution?
Calculation	calculate?
Verification	monitor the course of solution?

Table 6.5. The CSA Multisensory Technique

C oncrete	Use hands-on manipulatives.
S emiconcrete	Use and create pictures.
A bstract	Pair numerical symbols with concrete and semiconcrete aids.

numbers are not systematically paired with the concrete aids. Some students need the teacher to make those connections explicit.

2. **Be aware that some students may get confused and disorganized when learning about the various problem-solving strategies they are supposed to learn.** Figure 6.11 is a list of problem-solving strategies (Coburn, Hoogeboom, & Goodnow, 1989) that are currently the focus of many elementary and middle school math curricula. Students with learning disabilities and attention deficit disorders (ADD) need to be taught how to select an appropriate strategy and how to organize the information in a systematic way. Graphic organizers, especially those students create themselves with your help, are effective tools for learning how to solve math word problems systematically.

3. **Use graphic organizers, and teach students how to create their own graphic organizers.** Some students can organize information from a word problem or a table without your help. The work sample shown in Figure 6.12 is a good example of work of a second-grade student who has a strength in this area. However, some students need to be taught how to organize relevant information, especially students who have LD and/or ADD.

   Figure 6.13 is an example of a fourth-grade student's personally designed graphic organizer that was meaningful to him. The Ninja Math graphic reminded him to take the time to plan and to be systematic in his approach. After a while, he began to internalize and visualize his organizational strategy so that he no longer had to draw out the entire figure.

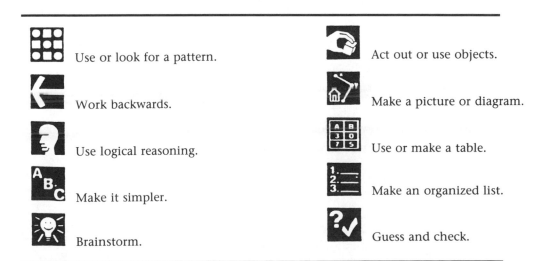

Use or look for a pattern.		Act out or use objects.	
Work backwards.		Make a picture or diagram.	
Use logical reasoning.		Use or make a table.	
Make it simpler.		Make an organized list.	
Brainstorm.		Guess and check.	

Figure 6.11. A list of problem-solving strategies for math curricula. From *The Problem Solver with Calculators*, by Coburn et al., 1989, Mountain View, CA: Creative Publications.

Figure 6.12. Work sample of a second-grade student showing how the student organized information from a word problem. From *TOPS Calculator Problem Deck IV* by C. Greenes, G. Immerzerl, L. Schulman, and R. Spungin, 1989, Palo Alto, CA: Dale Seymour Publications. Copyright 1989 by Dale Seymour Publications. Reprinted with permission.

Figure 6.14 is another example of a student-created organizer that helped a student to solve word problems systematically. Keith, whose case is described at the end of this chapter, created a RAPM strategy, which stands for:

R = READ & RAP (Read the problem and repeat in your own words.)

A = ART (Represent the problem by drawing a diagram.)

P = PLAN & PREDICT (Think of a plan for solving the problem, and predict the answer.)

M = MELVIN the calculator (Use a calculator; in this case the student named his calculator Melvin.)

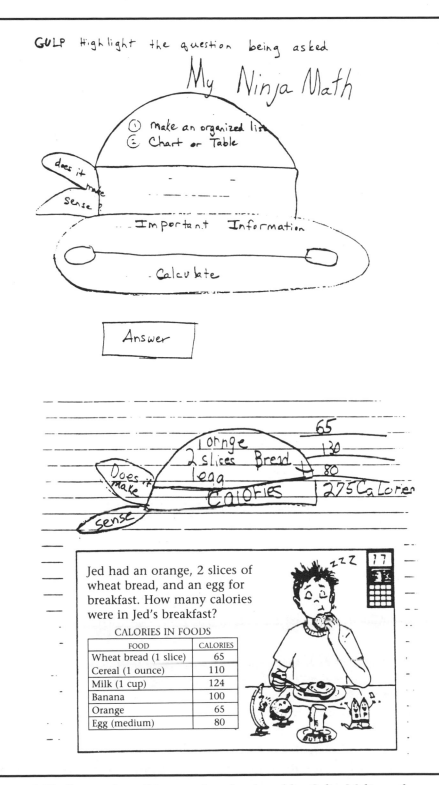

Figure 6.13. Personal graphic organizer developed by Colin Meltzer, then a fourth-grade student.

A restaurant manager has 144 flowers. She wants to put the same number on each of 24 tables. How many flowers can she put on each table?

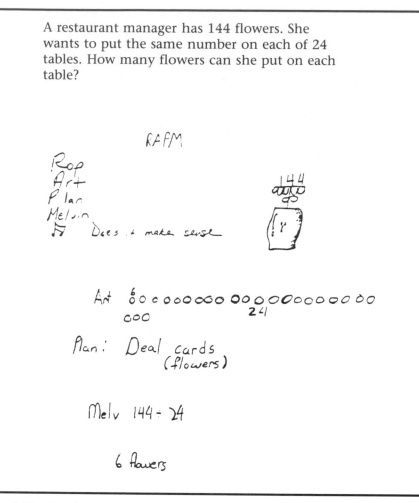

Figure 6.14. Another example of a student-created organizer to help solve word problems.

Then Keith sings to himself, asking the question, "Does it make sense?"

Many students, like Keith, rely on writing the RAPM acrostic out each time they begin a new problem. Over time, students internalize the process and need to write out the steps only when they encounter a more difficult problem. For example, the RAPM strategy can be applied multiple times to help solve multi-step problems. See excerpts from Keith's math strategy notebook in Figure 6.14 for samples of this strategy used in this way.

4. **Develop personal checklists of questions that students should ask themselves when solving problems or checking their work.** Students often forget to check their work, and students with learning problems often do not know how to check their work systematically. You can assist them by helping them create their own personalized checklists of questions that tap typical errors. The following is an example of a math checklist:

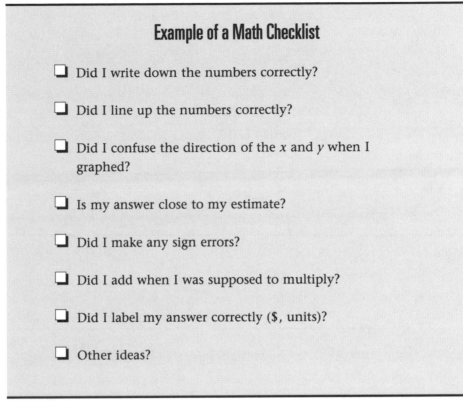

Example of a Math Checklist

❏ Did I write down the numbers correctly?

❏ Did I line up the numbers correctly?

❏ Did I confuse the direction of the *x* and *y* when I graphed?

❏ Is my answer close to my estimate?

❏ Did I make any sign errors?

❏ Did I add when I was supposed to multiply?

❏ Did I label my answer correctly ($, units)?

❏ Other ideas?

© 1996 PRO-ED, Inc.

Algebra

At the middle and high school levels, all students, and students with learning difficulties in particular, benefit from some mnemonic device to remember how to factor polynomials. Typically, FOIL is taught, an acrostic for F=first, O=outside term, I=inside term, L=last term. Some students cannot remember the FOIL trick, and they need a more meaningful and visual cue. Figure 6.15 demonstrates FACE, which is an effective strategy in that students can focus on the algebraic sign of the middle terms, which is a troublesome area for most students. Note that the three forms of factoring are summarized for the students in a list form that also utilizes visual cues. You can write this list on the overhead or on the board, and the students can copy it into their math strategy notebooks.

Geometry

In geometry, students often confuse the multiple attributes of various geometric shapes. By developing flow diagrams and lists with your students, you can help them understand the interrelationships among the various geometric shapes.

Some of the new textbooks are providing diagrams like the one in Figure 6.16. However, it is especially effective if you develop the diagram with your students as an organizing framework rather than just giving them the diagram as another memorization task.

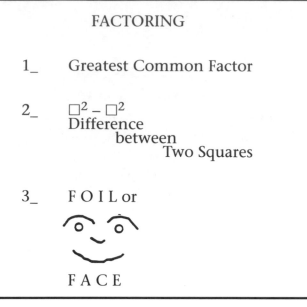

FACTORING

1_   Greatest Common Factor

2_ $\square^2 - \square^2$
       Difference
              between
                   Two Squares

3_   F O I L or

F A C E

Figure 6.15. Three forms of factoring: FACE, an effective strategy to prevent typical sign errors.

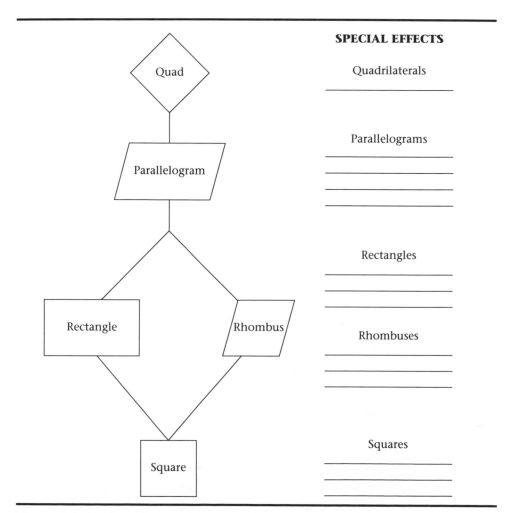

SPECIAL EFFECTS

Quad

Parallelogram

Rectangle   Rhombus

Square

Quadrilaterals
_____

Parallelograms
_____
_____
_____

Rectangles
_____
_____

Rhombuses
_____
_____

Squares
_____
_____

Figure 6.16. A flow diagram for learning geometric shapes.

Figure 6.17 is another example of how a graphic organizer can be used; but this time, a new concept and set of part–whole relationships are developed using manipulatives (geoboard and elastics), pictures (diagrams of geometric shapes), and language (mathematical symbols representing the relationships). Building on prior knowledge is critical.

Use of Management Techniques

Management techniques help individualize students within the context of a large, heterogeneous classroom. Some techniques are as follows:

- Math strategy notebooks
- Math rings
- Focus cards
- Strategy time
- Practice labs
- Individual math packets

Area of Parallelogram ????

1. Prior knowledge

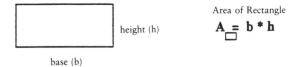

2. Use geoboard: What is area of triangle?

3. Can we turn rectangle into parallelogram?

4. Use number examples.

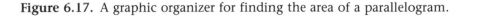

Figure 6.17. A graphic organizer for finding the area of a parallelogram.

1. **Develop math strategy notebooks for all of your students.** How can you possibly remember each student's math goals? Math strategy notebooks are especially useful in the classroom and/or small group settings for translating educational plan goals into student language. Students can identify and store their own math goals on "focus cards," and they can document newly learned strategies and examples in sections related to their goals. For example, the notebook may contain a section on automatic recall for math facts, problem-solving strategies, and telling time. Focus cards and math rings can be stored right in the students' notebooks. By doing so, the students and teachers are continually reminded of their math goals and strategies. Math strategy notebooks may include all of the following:

   - Instructional goals

   - Focus cards

   - Math ring in pockets

   - Summary clouds

   - Golden rule and examples

   - My own advanced graphic organizers

   - Portfolios

2. **Use index cards to help students focus on their math goals** (see Figure 6.18).

3. **Enrich and stretch your advanced students' mathematical thinking.** Depending on your students' ages and your instructional goals, you can offer certain students curriculum extensions by introducing new math vocabulary, such as reciprocals and commutative property, and algebraic equations. During

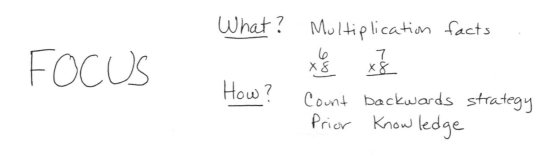

Figure 6.18. Index "focus" cards can be used to help students define their math goals.

practice labs, these students can work independently or collectively on an ongoing interdisciplinary math and science technology project. While other students are practicing skills and strategies in practice labs, you can spend some time interacting with those students who learn quickly and would benefit from additional challenges.

4. **Create a classroom climate that includes a balance of dialogue and independent thinking.**

   - Ask questions that have no wrong answers

   - Give students time to think about the problem for a couple of days.

   - Encourage them to discuss it with peers, friends, or family members.

   - Teach students how to listen to each other.

   - Encourage students to ask questions when they are unsure of a question or a line of discussion.

5. **Create flexible groupings based on the math goals and strategies that students are studying.** Although many teachers question whether it is possible to teach math to heterogeneous groups, many schools have adopted these classrooms. To balance the needs of your students, you can form flexible, homogeneous groups within a heterogeneous classroom. Rather than grouping students according to low, middle, and high skill levels, you can group them according to the math goals and strategies that they are studying. For example, the following groups may be formed: addition facts, multiplication facts, graphic organizers for problem solving, drawing diagrams for problem solving, problem-solving project groups. All of the students will benefit from exposure to all of these aspects of math instruction, but after a full class presentation, these groups can be formed to practice specific skills and strategies.

   Grouping students according to learning style strengths is another factor to consider when defining groups. By structuring time for practicing strategies (strategy time or practice lab), you will find that you have more time to interact with small groups of students while others can practice and problem-solve in small groups or work individually. Using math strategy notebooks and focus cards as your guides, strategy time and practice labs that last from 10 to 20 minutes can offer an effective use of time to individualize within your classroom.

6. **Set up math labs.** A common question asked by teachers is, "How can I orchestrate these groupings during math time?" Here is an example of how one teacher balanced her teaching. Three times a week, she taught to her heterogeneous class. Twice a week, she and another teacher grouped the children

according to skills and strategies for math lab. During that time, teachers were able to challenge the students who needed curriculum extensions. At the same time, the other teacher combined the class to teach those students who needed more practice and reinforcement on particular skills or strategies. By teaming up with a teacher in this way, you can address a wider range of needs in a systematic way.

7. **Individualize homework.** Math lab, strategy time, or practice lab are opportune times to individualize homework. Some teachers like to have one core assignment for all of their students, and then they add on additional types of problems according to the strategy groupings. Other teachers prefer to offer completely different assignments depending on the math goals or strategies studied by different groups. For example, the math fact recall group would get an assignment based on their math goal for the week. The problem-solving project group may be taking home challenging problems related to their project. Some teachers have organized the various homework assignments using a color-coded system. For example, the students' focus cards are color-coded depending on their math goals, and two or three homework packets are color-coded to correspond to those goals. Sometimes, the teacher hands out colored construction paper to each student indicating which homework he or she should take home on a particular night.

8. **Individualize tests.** Tests may be prepared such that all students are required to answer questions from a certain section of the test. Additional sections are provided to test progress on individual or small group goals. You may indicate by color or check mark the additional sections that you would like specific students to take. Collecting work samples (e.g., pages from math strategy notebooks that represent personal triumphs toward specific math goals) are an especially effective means of portfolio assessment. These portfolios can also be used for parent–teacher–student conferences.

   If you organize biweekly math labs where students are grouped according to ability on particular skills or strategies, then you can administer different tests at this time. Teachers can teach and test to homogeneous groups during math lab, and they can teach and test to heterogeneous groups during the other three periods of math during the week.

9. **Incorporate multisensory teaching techniques into your classroom presentations.** To address multiple learning profiles in the classroom, some teaching techniques are as follows:

Teaching Techniques to Address Multiple Learning Profiles

❏ Use colored chalk or colored markers to group like information.

❏ Provide large block graph paper to help students line up numbers correctly.

❏ Fold math paper into quadrants to provide one space for each problem.

❏ Combine multiple representations (e.g., concrete aids with pictures with numerical symbols).

❏ Link new concepts to prior knowledge.

❏ Model three-column note-taking and summary boxes.

❏ Build in systematic routines and questioning sequences.

❏ Use real-life examples to make math concepts meaningful (e.g., money).

❏ Teach students how to estimate and to use this strategy to check their work.

❏ List questions that students should ask themselves as they solve problems.

❏ Develop a personal checklist for checking their work.

❏ Balance verbal discussions with visual models and hands-on experiences.

❏ Use step-by-step question-answer routines.

❏ Teach students how to look for patterns across examples.

❏ Encourage students to paraphrase word problems aloud.

❏ Give students extra time to practice new strategies or procedures.

❏ Stay attuned to those students who "don't get it."

❏ Give those students on-the-spot tutorial so they can keep up with class.

❏ Follow up group lessons with individualized extra help sessions for those students who need it.

❏ Other ideas?

Usually, your students will have a wide range of abilities and disabilities. For a group lesson, you can incorporate the use of multiple teaching techniques simultaneously to meet the diverse needs of all your students. Then, students with difficulties will likely need extra help from you or your classroom aide (if you are lucky enough to have one).

Concluding Remarks

In today's math classrooms, we need to continually strive toward achieving balance. We must continually question ourselves:

- Are we balancing rote instruction with meaningful problem solving?

- Are we addressing the needs of the students who are slow processors as well as providing curriculum challenges for the mathematically gifted student?

- Are we using multisensory instruction—balancing oral lecture and classroom discourse with visual models and hands-on opportunities?

- Are we balancing the teaching of math skills with the teaching of math strategies?

In today's heterogeneous classrooms with minimal teacher training and classroom supports, the challenge is greater than ever to meet the diverse needs of your students. We hope this manual will provide you with some survival skills and practical teaching techniques in mathematics that will assist you in accomplishing your goals for your students.

A Math Case Study

Keith was referred for a specific mathematics evaluation when he was 9 years old. He was first evaluated for learning problems as a repeating first-grade student. Keith was found to possess above average to superior intelligence. He was diagnosed with a learning disability and ADDnoH (attention deficit disorder without hyperactivity). During this initial evaluation, Keith demonstrated particular strengths in abstract verbal reasoning and recall of structured visual material; in contrast, weaknesses were evidenced in his attention to details, sequencing, automatic memory, systematic analytic reasoning, and ability to follow multistep directions. The second mathematics-focused evaluation identified processing strengths in classifying and categorizing both linguistic and nonlinguistic knowledge. On the other hand, Keith demonstrated significant weaknesses in analysis, memory, sequencing, and completion of patterns. Keith's automatic recall for letters and numbers was poor, and complex tasks involving multiple details overwhelmed him.

These findings helped to explain the difficulties Keith had been experiencing in learning mathematics. His general lack of automaticity and ability to "shift sets" interfered with his ability to memorize math facts, represent number concepts with manipulatives, and translate words into numerical representations. Specifically, shifting between linguistic and numerical processing compromised Keith's strong logical reasoning skills. In addition, Keith's attentional deficits resulted in many impulsive responses and poor self-monitoring strategies.

Selective mainstreaming with close communication and cooperation between the classroom teacher and a special educator was recommended. In this manner, Keith would receive frequent individualized instruction and review.

As is evident from Table 6.6, goals for Keith included increasing his automaticity for recalling number facts and helping him develop systematic approaches when solving word problems. It was recommended that Keith be given structured, multisensory, and contextual learning opportunities in mathematics. These techniques would help Keith access his logical reasoning strengths. In particular, it was suggested that Keith be encouraged to work to improve his automatic recall for math facts.

Specific instructional strategies included the identification of stratofacts and clueless facts to construct personalized fact rings, tables, and other graphic organizers. It was also recommended that Keith be taught specific structured routines (e.g., RAPM) to develop meaningful math problem-solving strategies. In conjunction with developing personalized visual representations of useful strategies (see Figure 6.19 for illustrations of Keith's work), it was recommended that Keith be taught to construct a math strategy notebook as a metacognitive aid and as a means of providing ongoing documentation of his developing mathematical strategies. Teaching techniques such as CSA were suggested to help Keith to proceed from concrete to semiconcrete to abstract mathematical reasoning. Finally, Keith's difficulties in switching flexibly between verbal and numerical representations justified the use of computational bypasses (e.g., calculators) in complex problem-solving situations.

Table 6.6. Case Study: Math

Processes	Educational Manifestations	Recommendations[a]
STRENGTHS		
Abstract reasoning	Accurate problem solving when tasks are well structured Strengths in analyzing oral information Strong classification and categorization skills Able to apply general rules appropriately	Specify sequences for solving problems Brainstorm multiple strategies and solutions Restate problems in his own words

(continued)

Table 6.6. *Continued*

Processes	Educational Manifestations	Recommendations
Visual processing	Good performance when solving visually formatted problems	Draw pictures of word problems Teach use of graphic organizers
	Artistically talented	Color-code written information in math problems

WEAKNESSES

Processes	Educational Manifestations	Recommendations
Automatic memory	Cannot remember math facts	Math fact drill with emphasis on remembering strategies (e.g., one-up rule, doubles, math fact families, etc.) Use math strategy notebook, fact rings Use calculator and/or chart of "troublesome facts" when concentrating on word problem solutions Direct instruction in estimation and rounding Teach facts in meaningful contexts (e.g., rhymes, mnemonics) Instruction in creating procedural lists and charts Extensive spiraled instruction
Sequencing	Lacks systematic approaches to solving word problems Difficulty performing multi-step procedures	Use of focus rings for problem-solving strategies Teach structured routines (e.g., RAPM)
Flexibility	Difficulty translating words into numerical representations	Minimize reading demands Teach use of graphic organizers, tables, checklists for self-monitoring
Attention	Distractible	Preferential seating near teacher and/or away from distractions Reduce amount of text per page
	Attacks problem-solving impulsively	Break down multistep directions and repeat if necessary
Self-monitoring	Does not recognize own computational errors	Create and refer to self-check lists

[a]All of the suggested instructional strategies can be integrated into the regular classroom incorporating techniques of flexible groupings and practice labs.

FOCUS

What? Multiplication facts

$$\begin{array}{cc} 6 & 7 \\ \times 8 & \times 8 \end{array}$$

How? Count backwards strategy
Prior Knowledge

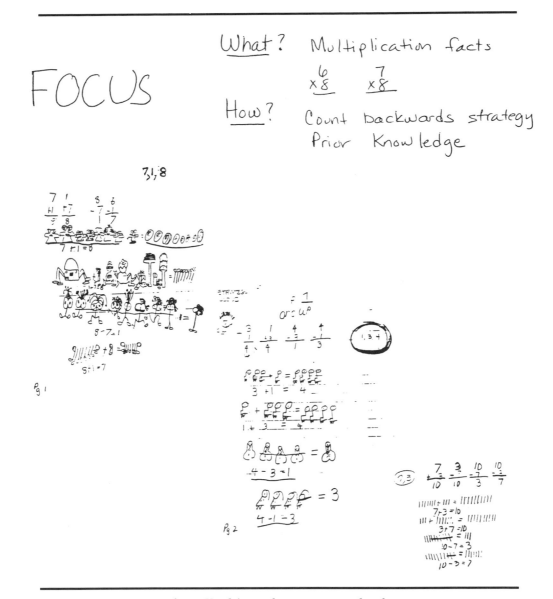

Figure 6.19. Excerpts from Keith's math strategy notebook.

Chapter 7

Strategy Use Across Content Areas

Why Teach Strategies in the Content Areas?

Strategy instruction within the content areas is especially important in the intermediate and later grades. Grades 4, 7, and the onset of high school represent critical transition points in every student's education. When students reach the fourth grade, the emphasis in classrooms shifts from learning to read to reading to learn. In addition, at each critical transition point, students are expected to function more independently, and a greater emphasis is placed on complex thinking and problem-solving skills. Many teachers assume that their students have already acquired the basic reading, writing, and organizational skills necessary for success in the content areas. However, this may not be the case for students with learning difficulties. For these students, success in the content areas depends on continued strategy instruction.

Shouldn't All Students Already Know How to Learn?

Because most teachers were efficient students, it may be difficult for them to understand that many students with learning difficulties need explicit instruction in study and test-taking strategies. Furthermore, whereas successful students modify their strategy use to fit the task demands, students with learning difficulties need direct strategy instruction. For example, efficient learners employ different strategies when reading an English novel than when reading a science text. In contrast, students with learning difficulties do not automatically shift strategies to match the requirements of different assignments. Their lack of flexibility in applying strategies may often impede their progress in the content areas.

In What Areas Do Students with Learning Difficulties Need Explicit Instruction?

Some examples of areas in which students with learning difficulties may need explicit instruction are the following:

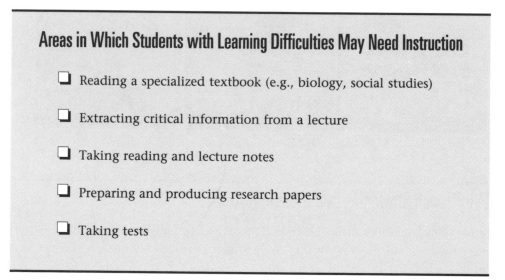

Areas in Which Students with Learning Difficulties May Need Instruction

❏ Reading a specialized textbook (e.g., biology, social studies)

❏ Extracting critical information from a lecture

❏ Taking reading and lecture notes

❏ Preparing and producing research papers

❏ Taking tests

Students with learning difficulties experience a "double jeopardy" when they enter the middle and upper grades. This situation arises as they attempt to master content without having previously mastered the basic skills or strategies that are the foundation for this new and challenging stage of learning. In other words, a gap exists between the students' skills and the demands of the curriculum. Unfortunately, this gap often continues to widen as students progress through the middle and high school grades.

How Can the Gap Be Bridged?

Through specific strategy instruction, you have the tools to enhance each student's opportunity to master the material in your course. By gaining a thorough understanding of the demands of your curriculum and your teaching style, you can empower your students with the strategies they need to succeed in your class. Strategies are best taught in context. That means you are in an ideal position to teach your students not only *what* to learn, but also *how* to learn in your classroom. Remember, *make no assumptions* about the skills and strategies your students bring to your course material.

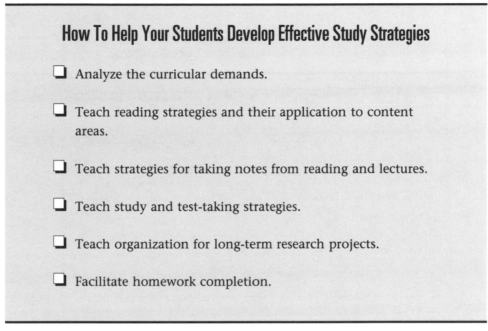

How To Help Your Students Develop Effective Study Strategies

❑ Analyze the curricular demands.

❑ Teach reading strategies and their application to content areas.

❑ Teach strategies for taking notes from reading and lectures.

❑ Teach study and test-taking strategies.

❑ Teach organization for long-term research projects.

❑ Facilitate homework completion.

Will the Same Strategies Work for All Subject Areas?

The strategies needed by students with learning difficulties in each class will depend on the following:

- The student's profile of strengths and weaknesses

- The specific course material

- The teacher's style of instruction

- The method of assessment

Analyze the Demands of Your Course

By analyzing your course demands and your teaching style, you can identify the skills necessary for success in your content area class. In other words, it is important to understand the fit between your course material, teaching style, and assessment techniques and the learning profiles of your students. There are numerous steps to understanding your course demands and translating them to your students. These steps include an examination of your style of teaching, your textbook, and your grading system.

1. **Examine your teaching style.**

   a. *Lectures.* Do you present most material in lecture format? Lectures often make up close to 50% of the instructional procedures in content area classes at the middle and high school levels. Students with learning difficulties often have difficulty understanding lectures because the information is presented through a single sensory modality. These students may need modifications in those classes that rely heavily on lecture presentations.

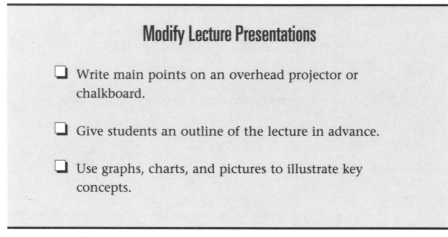

   ### Modify Lecture Presentations

   ❑ Write main points on an overhead projector or chalkboard.

   ❑ Give students an outline of the lecture in advance.

   ❑ Use graphs, charts, and pictures to illustrate key concepts.

   © 1996 PRO-ED, Inc.

   b. *Independent reading assignments.* In contrast to oral lectures, how much independent reading is expected of students in your class? In many content area classes, class discussions and tests are based on textbook reading assignments. Some students with learning difficulties may be unable to extract critical information from a textbook. Reading guides and other strategies may provide the tools these students need to comprehend and retain the information from a textbook reading assignment. (See the reading strategies section of this chapter and Chapter 4 of this book, on reading comprehension, for detailed suggestions.)

2. **Examine your textbook.** Textbooks continue to be an integral component of most classroom instruction. Therefore, success in the classroom often depends on a student's ability to master textbook reading assignments. Teachers and students need a thorough understanding of their textbooks. Further, students need strategies for comprehending material presented in this format. Although the readability level of a textbook is important, many other critical components influence the selection and effective use of textbooks in the classroom. Table 7.1 outlines methods for reviewing and using textbooks.

   Once you understand your text from the perspective of the learner, share that information with your students. Take your students through the first reading assignment as you model strategies that will help them comprehend the material. Preview important vocabulary words that students will encounter in their reading. Discuss reading assignments in advance. Integrate the textbook with strategy instruction, and you will empower your students to become independent and confident learners.

Table 7.1. Methods for Using Textbooks in the Classroom

Is your textbook within a readable level for the group of students you are teaching?
- Use the Fry Readability Index (see Appendix 1).

Is there a study guide that could be used in conjunction with the text?
- Use the study guide to supplement the text.
- Develop outlines or reading guides to accompany text.

How is your text organized?
- Discuss the structure of the text with your students.
- Brainstorm with them for the most effective ways to handle reading assignments
- Be explicit about clues to reading, such as important vocabulary words highlighted in boldface, clearly delineated sections, main ideas accented in headings or in the margins, study questions.

Are important vocabulary words highlighted in boldface?
- Preview the vocabulary with the students.
- Direct students to pay close attention to boldface words.
- Distribute lists of important words if they are not explicitly highlighted in the text.

Are the questions at the end of the chapter good prereading tools for the students?
- Encourage the students to read the questions before they begin the reading assignment.

Note. See Ciborowski (1992) for textbook review form.

3. **Examine your grading system.** In secondary school, almost half of each student's grade is based on test performance (Putnam, Deshler, & Schumaker, 1993). Some students may grasp the content of a course, but lack the skills they need to demonstrate their knowledge, especially in written form. It is critical for students to understand your grading system. It is also crucial for them to have many ways to demonstrate mastery of your material. It is often helpful to include students in the decision-making process as you review different grading systems. This allows them to become more involved and to develop some ownership over the process.

Points to Consider When Examining Your Grading System

❑ Be explicit about the grading policy.

❑ Consider using multilevel grading (e.g., mechanics, organization, and content).

❑ Give credit for class participation.

❑ Evaluate students' performance in a variety of ways (e.g., oral tests, special projects).

4. Explain the curricular demands to your students. Students with learning difficulties are not efficient at picking up subtle clues about classroom demands. In addition, they have difficulty prioritizing their efforts. Once these students understand the particular strategies required to succeed in a specific class, they will be more focused, less frustrated, and more likely to experience success with the content material. If your goal is mastery of the material, give your students the clues they need to solve the mystery of learning in your classroom. Success with the material and the strategies you show students will spur their motivation in your course.

Teach Reading Strategies and Their Content Area Application

Students with learning difficulties often have particular difficulty reading content material. This is because they may have poor reading strategies. The reading strategies students must employ to gain meaning from text will differ slightly for each subject, as the language used to communicate concepts varies among content areas. Students with learning difficulties often struggle to vary their use of reading strategies. That is why it is critical for these students to receive reading strategy instruction within each content area. Specific suggestions for reading strategies are listed in Chapter 4.

Teach Note-Taking Strategies

The emphasis on lectures and independent reading assignments in the upper grades means that students must develop efficient note-taking strategies. Note-taking strategies are important for all students and are particularly critical for students with poor organizational skills and language deficits. The most effective method for teaching note taking will differ according to the learning profile of each student. You can instruct your students in a variety of note-taking techniques within the context of your course, including the following:

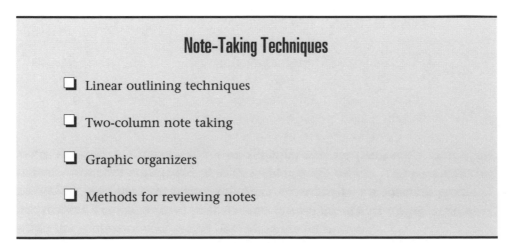

Note-Taking Techniques

❏ Linear outlining techniques

❏ Two-column note taking

❏ Graphic organizers

❏ Methods for reviewing notes

1. **Teach linear outlining techniques.** Linear outlining is the most commonly used method. However, many students have not received explicit instruction in outlining. For students with learning difficulties, explicit and repeated instruction and practice are essential. Outlines help students to focus on the material.

   a. Begin by distributing a skeletal outline, which students complete as you lecture or as they read.

   b. Distribute the outline in advance so students have ample time to read it.

   c. Model the outlining procedure on an overhead projector.

   d. Allow students to compare their outlines to yours.

   e. Gradually, fade the support as students begin to assume more responsibility for their learning.

2. **Teach two-column note taking.** This technique may be an effective strategy for students who have difficulty differentiating main ideas from details. Two-column notes are also helpful as study guides, because they are formatted for self-testing (see Figure 7.1 for an example).

   a. Fold a sheet of paper in half lengthwise.

   b. During the lecture, the student records information on the right side of the sheet.

   c. After class, the student groups like information into categories or main questions.

   d. The student then records the main ideas on the left side of the paper.

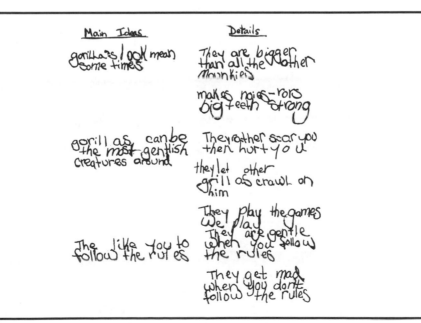

Figure 7.1. An example of two-column notes.

3. **Teach students to use graphic organizers.** Graphic organizers are especially helpful for students with strong visual-spatial skills. Examples can be found in Chapters 4 and 5 of this book.

   a. Use graphics to illustrate the connections among ideas so that students can visualize the concepts presented.

   b. Use mapping and webbing strategies (see Chapters 4 and 5).

4. **Teach methods for reviewing notes.** Depending on their learning styles, students benefit from some or all of the following strategies:

   a. Allow time during or after class for students to discuss their questions about their notes (critical for all students).

   b. Students can . . .

      —rewrite their notes.

      —write down questions about the notes.

      —recite notes.

      —reread notes.

      —tape-record and listen to notes.

5. **Consider modifications to traditional classroom note taking.** For a small number of students, note taking is particularly difficult. Note taking requires listening, extracting critical information, and writing at the same time. Students with weaknesses in any one of these areas can become easily overloaded, especially when they are required to perform multiple tasks. Therefore, the following modifications are useful:

   a. Allow students to tape-record lectures and develop outlines from the recording.

   b. Allow the student to choose a friend who will act as secretary.

   c. Give students copies of your lecture notes.

   d. Appoint one strong note-taker a month to be the scribe for weaker note-takers.

   e. Tape-record your lectures and allow students to borrow your tapes.

6. **Consider various note-taking styles.** It is important to introduce your students to each of these note-taking techniques. By demonstrating all of these possibilities, you will discover that different students prefer different note-taking methods.

   a. Introduce one note-taking technique per month and provide time for practice.

b. Encourage students to discuss methods they prefer to use.

c. Develop templates for each method and make these available in bins.

d. Permit students to select the template that suits their learning style.

Teach Study Strategies

Students with learning and attentional difficulties often require explicit instruction in study strategies beginning in the early grades and continuing in the later grades. Many students implicitly learn how to study, but others need explicit strategy instruction, additional support, or modifications. In fact, all students benefit from instruction in study strategies.

1. **Teach general study strategies.** Students with learning difficulties often have trouble organizing information into a logical sequence and differentiating salient information from details. Therefore, many students with learning difficulties do not know how to study for a test and need to be taught specific strategies for each content area class.

General Study Strategies

❏ Make flash cards for vocabulary words by putting the vocabulary word on one side and the definition on the back. Self-test by reading the vocabulary word and saying the definition aloud. Using both writing and speaking is a multisensory way of reinforcing the vocabulary.

❏ Create charts when studying detailed content. For example, time lines are useful for remembering the sequence of events in a history or social studies class. The visual aids will help to reinforce the order of the events.

❏ Develop a key word–question–answer review sheet by dividing the paper into three columns and writing an important (key) word in the first column, a specific question in the second, and the answer in the third. The key words will help students remember the questions and the answers. Again, students can self-test by answering questions aloud.

❏ Create their own tests like the one expected from you, their teacher. Also, tell students to take the tests themselves!

---

2. **Teach use of study guides.** As previously discussed, separating the main ideas from less salient details is extremely difficult for students with learning difficulties. Therefore, study guides provide very helpful concrete guidance. Teacher-created study guides supply students with direction and organization for studying. It is obviously important to remember to use the information given to the students in the study guides when creating the tests. Study guides can take several formats, including the following examples:

Examples of Study Guides

❑ *Questions:* If your textbook supplies helpful questions at the chapter ends, these can be pointed out to students. Otherwise, create a list of your own questions.

❑ *Vocabulary/concept lists:* These lists supply students with important terms or concepts to focus their studying. The student's job is to find information to define or describe these. The lists work especially well in science, social studies, and foreign language classes.

❑ *Graphic organizers:* Visually organized information will help students associate like ideas.

© 1996 PRO-ED, Inc.

Teach Test-Taking Strategies

Students with learning difficulties frequently experience problems with tests, especially multiple-choice and timed tests. Problems are often identified only after frequent discrepancies are discovered between the students' high grades for in-class work and their low scores on standardized tests. The performance of students with learning difficulties often varies depending on the test format, which may include fill-in-the-blank procedures, matching, cloze procedures, essays, and traditional multiple-choice formats. Students with learning difficulties often experience confusion when the test format differs from the format of the original text. The vocabulary used in the tests may also be problematic. Multiple-choice tests are particularly problematic for students with learning difficulties because of the emphasis on detecting salience, isolating critical information, ignoring less relevant details, and analyzing complex language. The layout of the record forms is often confusing, because many of these students experience spatial organization problems.

To prepare students for tests you can use some of the following procedures:

- Provide explicit study guides that describe exactly what students will be expected to know for the test. Suggestions for study guides can be found in the previous section.

- Give samples of previous tests so that students have models for the language and question types you use.

- Take your students through a mock test, demonstrating the various levels of information they will need to answer the different types of questions you may use.

- Show them how to prepare for each type of test question (e.g., review strategies for multiple choice, true/false, fill-in-the-blank, and outlining for possible essays).

During testing, all students could benefit from additional teacher support and modeling of test-taking strategies. Assist students during tests by doing the following:

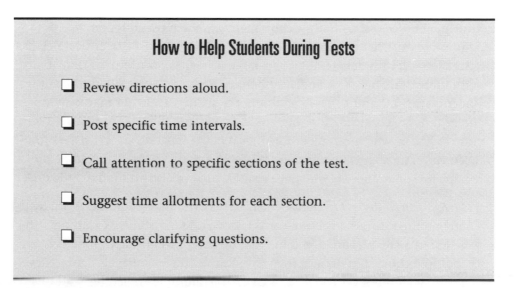

How to Help Students During Tests

❑ Review directions aloud.

❑ Post specific time intervals.

❑ Call attention to specific sections of the test.

❑ Suggest time allotments for each section.

❑ Encourage clarifying questions.

Be certain that you have allotted sufficient time for students to complete your test. A good guideline is to triple the amount of time it takes for you to complete your own test.

Test questions usually fall into three categories:

- *Recognition tests:* Multiple choice, true/false, matching

- *Recall tests:* Fill in the blank, list, label, diagram, define

- *Production tests:* Word problems, essays, short answer, computation

Each type of question necessitates the application of different processes or skills. A student's performance on a test will sometimes depend on the test format. By using a combination of question types including recall, recognition, and production, you can provide opportunities for students with various learning styles to show what they know. It is especially important that students with LD and ADD understand what is required to answer each type of question.

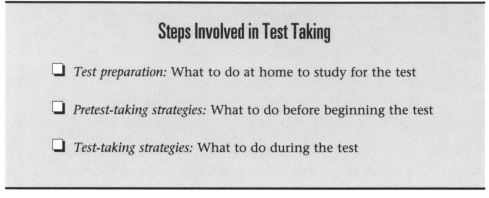

Steps Involved in Test Taking

❏ *Test preparation:* What to do at home to study for the test

❏ *Pretest-taking strategies:* What to do before beginning the test

❏ *Test-taking strategies:* What to do during the test

1. **Multiple-choice tests.** Multiple-choice tests are the most common type of recognition tests. They require students to detect salience, isolate critical details, ignore less relevant details, analyze complex language, conform to time limits, and differentiate between similar responses. These skills are often difficult for students with LD and ADD. In addition, the spatial layouts of many multiple-choice tests are confusing for some students, because the lines of type are often close together, which can be distracting. When a separate answer page is provided, an extra step is involved in transferring the answers. This can be problematic for some students who have visual-spatial or organizational difficulties.

   a. *Preparation strategies for multiple-choice tests.* In multiple-choice tests, students are required to recognize the correct answer. Many students read only the required material, and then think that they have studied appropriately for a multiple-choice test. In fact, they have learned the material at a surface level but not to the level of recall. Answers on multiple-choice tests are often similar, which may create confusion for students who study only to the level of recognition. For these reasons, it is important to teach students how to study effectively. Some techniques for studying to the level of recall in multiple-choice tests include the following:

      • Teach students to make up and complete their own multiple-choice questions using the information from their notes or in their texts. They could also exchange tests with a partner.

      • Remind students to answer recognition questions at the ends of chapters.

      • Teach students to use strategies such as mnemonic devices to memorize lists, dates, and vocabulary terms.

b. *Pretest strategies for multiple-choice tests.* To help students with LD and ADD avoid feeling overwhelmed by the format and length of many multiple-choice tests, the following pretest-taking strategies can be explicitly taught and modeled by the teacher:

- Tell students to skim the layout of the test. Is there a separate answer sheet?

- Give students the option of using index cards or rulers to track along if there is a separate answer sheet.

- Tell students to read directions carefully to find out if there is a penalty for guessing. This may not be particularly applicable in the classroom; however, points are deducted on the SATs for guessing.

- Alert students to important instructional words, such as, "Choose the statement that is *not* correct," "Which of the following occurred *after* 1945?" or "What is the *closest* answer to the problem 658 + 789 =?" Tell students to underline these words when reading the question initially.

- Teach students to break down multiple-choice questions by numbering each part for clarification and crossing out unimportant information.

Once students have completed the pretest-taking strategies, they should be explicitly taught how to approach the actual questions and how to best decide on an answer. Test-taking strategies for use during multiple-choice tests include the following:

Strategies for Multiple-Choice Tests

❑ Read all of the questions, answering only the ones students know first. Circle the questions they need to think about and return to these questions later.

❑ Read the question while covering up the answer choices. Students should answer the question first in their heads, then find the given answer that best matches their original response.

❑ Recognize that multiple-choice answers usually include a correct answer, an answer that is obviously wrong, and two answers that are close to the correct one. Teach students to cross out the choice that is wrong and to use a process of elimination to help limit the number of answer choices.

(continued)

❏ Recognize and use names, dates, and places in other questions as clues to help answer more difficult questions.

❏ Read the question-carrier phrase thoroughly with each answer to decide which one fits best. For example, if the question is:

> The first president of the United States was:
> a) Thomas Jefferson   b) Susan B. Anthony
> b) George Washington   d) Bill Clinton

read, "The first president of the United States was . . . Thomas Jefferson." Repeat this for each answer.

❏ Guess if students are not sure (if there is no penalty for guessing).

❏ Plan ahead to save time to check their answers.

❏ Change only those answers that students are certain are incorrect. Otherwise, it is usually smart to stay with the first response.

2. **Matching and true/false tests.** Matching tests require students to recognize connected ideas. Often, these tests are formatted as two lists in which the student must find the facts or ideas that are related. True/false tests are also widely used. Statements are usually presented to students, and they decide if the fact or idea is true or false. Another variation of this is to ask students to explain why the statement is true or false. In this way, students are required to support their answers with additional facts.

Test-taking strategies for matching tests and true/false tests include the following:

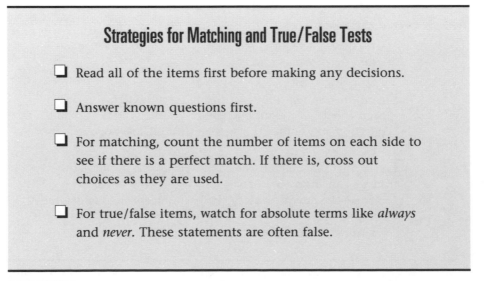

Strategies for Matching and True/False Tests

❏ Read all of the items first before making any decisions.

❏ Answer known questions first.

❏ For matching, count the number of items on each side to see if there is a perfect match. If there is, cross out choices as they are used.

❏ For true/false items, watch for absolute terms like *always* and *never*. These statements are often false.

3. **Fill-in-the-blank and short-answer tests.** Recall tests require students to remember disconnected facts or names rapidly and to use context clues. These tests also require strong visual memory. Fill-in-the-blank and labeling tests may be extremely difficult for those students with learning difficulties who have language-based word-retrieval problems, because it is difficult for them to recall specific names or words. Often, students with word-retrieval difficulties can "talk around" a word but are not able to supply an exact name. For example, these students may provide the function or description of an object but cannot produce the specific label. To address these specific weaknesses, it is important to teach these students specific test-taking strategies.

a. *Preparation strategies for fill-in-the-blank and short-answer tests.* It is important for fill-in-the-blank exams that students be able to recall specific words and details. Therefore, mnemonic devices are especially useful for students with learning difficulties. Mnemonic devices provide memory associations that help students remember important details. There are various forms of mnemonic devices, including acronyms, flash cards, rhymes, rhythms, and visual associations. An example of an acronym used for memorizing a list could be to use the first letter from each item to make a word or sentence (e.g., COPS uses the first letter of each proofreading step: Capitalization, Organization, Punctuation, Spelling). In addition, flash cards are useful for memorizing definitions or diagrams so that students can test themselves.

b. *Pretest-taking strategies for fill-in-the-blank and short-answer tests.* Recognition and recall tests are similar in that they both require a single "correct" answer. Many of the pretest-taking strategies listed in the multiple-choice section may be employed. In addition, the following suggestions are specifically applicable to recall tests:

Strategies for Short-Answer and Fill-in-the-Blank Tests

❑ For short-answer questions, write applicable mnemonic devices beside questions that require lists or definitions.

❑ For math problems, write the math procedure next to each problem.

❑ Read fill-in-the-blank questions completely, reread when filling in the target word, and read the completed sentence fully to self-check.

❑ For fill-in-the-blank tests, underline key information or context clues that will help to identify the target word.

(continued)

> ❑ Reread lists and paragraphs in response to short-answer questions to insure that students have written all of the information they know.
>
> ❑ Complete mathematical problems slowly and carefully. Check each step for computational errors.

4. **Essay tests.** Essay tests require that students plan ideas, organize information for a written presentation, prioritize statements, express ideas effectively, and demonstrate mastery of the writing process. Each of these individual requirements may be extremely difficult for students with learning disabilities. When these demands are combined in a testing situation with the anxiety resulting from a time limit, students often become overloaded. It is essential to teach the students explicitly how to approach essay questions.

   a. *Preparation strategies for essay tests.* Essay tests require students to learn broad content while focusing on salient ideas. The procedures for studying for essay tests can be very ambiguous and abstract. Both students with learning disabilities and normally achieving students may have difficulty organizing and studying for essay exams. This section includes selected strategies that students can use to study for essay tests.

   Essay tests emphasize the recall of broad topics with less attention to the memorization of supporting details. However, many students with learning difficulties do not know how to find the main ideas in texts and lectures. One concrete way of finding main ideas is the use of two-column note taking, especially in upper level texts, because this provides a structure for studying and organizing the material. After notes have been taken, students should group similar ideas together. This will help the students see patterns and associate ideas within the material. It is useful to model this for your students. Using the groups of information, students can write their own sample essay questions. They should practice answering these questions at home. These preparations will help them develop more effective writing skills and self-test their understanding of the material. Some strategies for finding main ideas in text have been previously described in the reading section of this chapter, including two-column note taking and questioning.

   b. *Pretest strategies for essay tests.* Because of the many facts and steps that need to be organized in an essay test, the most difficult task for many students is getting started. Following are some pretest-taking strategies teachers may use:

   • Skim over the test to determine what types of questions are on the test and how many points each question is worth.

- Plan how much time to spend on each question. Write the allotted time next to each question.

- Read each question carefully and analyze what is needed by doing the following:

  —Underline key words.

  —Break down multistep directions by numbering each step.

  —Develop a simple cutline.

  —Recognize the differences among key words (e.g., compare/contrast, enumerate, evaluate, describe, illustrate). (See Table 7.2 for examples of key words and their meanings.)

Since many students with learning difficulties struggle with vocabulary, they may need explicit instruction and practice with common key words used in essay tests. A chart such as the one in Table 7.2 may assist students in understanding the sometimes subtle differences in the meaning of key words. Once students understand the question, they will be more likely to demonstrate their knowledge of the material in the essay.

Here are some specific examples of various key words and the responses each requires:

- *Enumerate* the reasons for the Civil War means list the events that led to the Civil War.

- *Compare* the British system of government with the United States system means discuss the similarities.

Table 7.2. Key Words Used in Essay Questions

Key Word	Asks For	Meaning
State	Everything	Describe precise terms Reproduce definition easily
Discuss	Everything	Investigate by argument Give pros and cons
Summarize	Main ideas	Give brief account of a theme or principle
Contrast	Specific characteristics	Show the differences between two or more things
Explain	Specific characteristics	Clearly state and interpret details around something
Evaluate	Give your supported opinion	Appraise the value or usefulness of something using your opinion and examples

- *Describe* the process that results in the birth of identical twins means give a detailed account in which the order of events is critical.

c. *A note about essay outlines.* In addition to assistance with vocabulary, some students may need explicit structure when planning and organizing their responses to an essay question. Here are some examples of helpful organizers:

- For a "compare" question, ask students to divide the page in half and list side by side the individually comparable aspects of each topic. Students who learn visually may use Venn diagrams or other simple maps (see Appendix 3).

- Provide examples or lists of the vocabulary to be used when answering an essay question. Include transition words, compare/contrast vocabulary, and content vocabulary you expect your students to know and use in their answers.

- If you want students to describe a process sequentially, allow them to use some adaptation of the process organizer sheet displayed in Figure 7.2.

d. *Strategies to use during essay tests.* Getting started is usually the most difficult task for students. Therefore, most of the relevant strategies are described above. The following are strategies to teach students to use for essay exams. The critical issue is to provide the structure to help students self-direct their thinking and writing.

Describe a Process

Process to be described:_____

List the events in time order. _____   List the words you can use to help you
_____   move through the steps (e.g., *first, next,*
_____   *then*). _____
_____   _____
_____   _____
_____   _____

Questions to ask yourself:
1. Have you included all of the important events?
2. Are all the events in order? If not, number them in order.
3. Underline the key terms you must use in your answer.
4. Do you have enough move words to get you from begining to end?

Use this chart to guide and remind you as you write.

Figure 7.2. A process organizer sheet.

Essay Test Strategies

❑ On scrap paper, brainstorm (list) all ideas relating to the question or make an outline or chart.

❑ Prioritize by grouping similar information together and re-order items to be used by numbering them (#1 = first priority).

❑ *Elaborate* on each item listed: describe, tell *why*, add examples, compare, and so on.

❑ Check off every item used.

❑ Encourage students to refer back to their initial outlines many times and to avoid straying from the topic.

❑ Encourage students to monitor elapsed time on the board during the test. Suggest that they check the clock regularly; the teacher could record 5- to 10-minute intervals during the exam.

❑ Encourage students to self-question:

—Did I stay on the topic?

—Did I write down everything that I can remember?

—Does my map (list or chart) relate to the questions or directions?

—Did I list information I already knew about this topic?

—Did I arrange my ideas in the order that makes the most sense?

—Have I included all of the important events?

—Are the events in order? If not, number the paragraphs or sentences.

—Did I use the key terms required by the question?

—Did I use enough transition words so that the essay was cohesive?

—Did I proofread using mnemonic strategies if needed?

❑ Encourage students to proofread for changes and corrections using personalized checklists for problematic areas, such as spelling and grammar. Students could bring their checklists to class the day of the test for you to review, and they could use them during the test.

Finally, consider alternative ways to present essay questions. For example:

- Allow for practice and revision. Give your students many opportunities to practice answering an essay question, and consider grading the students based on their improvement. Each time students revise their answers, they enhance their knowledge of the material while gaining the appropriate skills.

- Give the students several possible or past questions along with charts and outlines to help them organize the material. This allows students to prepare their ideas before tests and to practice writing based on a model. This method actually facilitates review of more content than can be covered in a single exam, but beware of overloading students with an unreasonably long list of potential questions. A variation is to give students several essay questions to prepare, but actually give only a few on the test. For example, give the students five essay questions and ask only two of the questions on the actual exam.

5. **Testing modifications.** Some students may need additional support in combination with the strategies outlined in this chapter.

- Give students untimed tests. Some students with LD and ADD may process information slowly, which means that it takes longer for them to read, write, or think about the information on a test. Therefore, time restrictions add pressure and anxiety to an already stressful situation. Many times, students may know the information but are not able to complete the test due to lack of time.

- Permit students to take the test in a different setting such as the resource room. This will free the student from distractions in a room full of people and will allow the student to read questions aloud and "talk" through a question without disturbing others in the classroom. Students with reading difficulties may need to have test questions read aloud to them.

- Students with severe writing difficulties may benefit from the option to answer essay tests orally or to tape-record their answers. This will enable them to demonstrate their knowledge of the material.

Teach Organization of Research Projects

Research projects can seem overwhelming to students who often focus only on the final project that needs to be completed in a limited time period. It is important to emphasize the process of completing a research project as well as the final product. This can be accomplished by breaking the written research project into manageable steps, each with its own set of guidelines, deadlines, and grades. In this manner, you can assess the skills of your students at each step, track their progress, and teach specific strategies for problem areas.

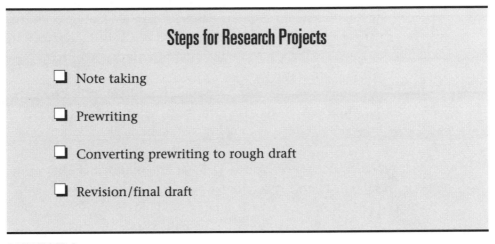

Steps for Research Projects

❑ Note taking

❑ Prewriting

❑ Converting prewriting to rough draft

❑ Revision/final draft

© 1996 PRO-ED, Inc.

1. **Note-taking techniques.** Many students in your class will instinctively know what is appropriate to write down for research notes. However, note taking may be very difficult for students with learning difficulties, because it combines several complex skills, including reading comprehension, isolating salient ideas, paraphrasing, and organizing information. Therefore, students should be explicitly taught to break note taking into several components. The following are some suggested strategies:

   • Help students establish topics and subtopics.

   • Check their notes to be certain that they are recording relevant information.

   • Give students practice in paraphrasing orally and in writing. Many students will not know how to restate a fact in their own words and may copy facts onto note cards. Therefore, the difference between paraphrasing (retelling in their own words) and plagiarism (copying) needs to be explicitly taught. Many students do not know the difference. Students can practice retelling facts.

   • Help students organize notes in a meaningful way by doing the following:

     —Write only one note on each separate index card.

     —Color-code the index cards by broad categories.

     —Show students how to manipulate the cards physically to form categories and to visualize relationships between ideas.

2. Prewriting

a. *Linear outlines.* Linear outlining helps many students organize their thoughts appropriately. However, some students may feel overwhelmed by the amount of time outlining takes. Therefore, teachers could give students the option of skipping this step if a student has demonstrated that he or she has arranged the note cards in a manner that could easily be converted into written paragraphs. Teachers may want to modify outlining in other ways to match a student's learning style.

If you would like your students to use linear outlines, it is essential to teach them how to approach and complete these. Many students have never had explicit instruction in outlining and are extremely confused by the format.

An adaptation of the traditional outline is one that includes topic sentences as headings. In this style, Roman numerals represent broad topics, and letters represent subtopics. Each letter or subtopic becomes a paragraph. To test this, the student substitutes the subtopic with a topic sentence and includes important details within this. This method of outlining is often very helpful for students with learning difficulties, because they can see how the outline helps organize the written paper. In addition, one of the most difficult aspects of writing is how to begin. This outline allows students to have a head start, because the topic sentences are already written. The following is an example of a linear outline:

Climates

I. *Introduction*—What is a climate?
II. *Desert*
    A. *Temperature*—A desert is a dry and hot place.
    B. *Living Things*—Specialized plants and animals live in the desert.
       1. Plants
       2. Animals
III. *Rain Forest*
    A. *Temperature*—Rain forests are often very hot and wet.
    B. *Living Things*—Plants and animals that live in the rain forest are adapted to that environment.
       1. Plants
       2. Animals
IV. *Conclusion*—What are the similarities and differences between a rain forest and a desert?

b. *Semantic maps.* For those students who are more visual, a graphic "outline" may be more beneficial than the verbal overload of a more traditional linear outline. Semantic maps are visual representations that show how ideas are related. For a research project, similar ideas could be grouped together on the map. (Semantic maps are described in detail in Chapter 4.)

c. *Organization of note cards.* For some students, outlining may be an unnecessary and time-consuming step. These students may benefit from grouping note cards into categories. Students can compose directly from their group of notes.

3. **Prewriting to rough draft.** Once students have written or formed some type of outline, they need to use this prewriting tool to begin writing a rough draft. Many students with learning difficulties do not know how to use their prewriting tools to organize their writing or how to convert this to a rough draft. Specific instruction and modeling of this process is often quite helpful. (More information about the writing process and the anatomy of a paper is provided in Chapter 5.)

4. **Revision to final draft.** Many students are not aware that the revising and editing steps are an essential part of writing a research paper. Many believe that the assignment has been completed when a rough draft has been written. Explain to students what is entailed in editing and revising; many will believe that the process refers to checking spelling and punctuation. However, an essential part of revision is reorganization of words within sentences and a more global reorganization of ideas in sentences and paragraphs.

   The process of revising can also be overwhelming for a student. Therefore, it is essential to explain and model the process of revising and editing for the students. Brainstorm with your students a list of areas that need to be addressed when revising. These lists will vary dependent on the grade level of the students—for example, high school students will probably have a longer, more detailed list than fourth-grade students. As mentioned previously, each step in a research paper can be examined and graded independently as a multistep grading strategy. In this manner, students will hand in rough drafts and a final copy for you to see their revisions. (For specific examples and further explanation of revision strategies, refer to the writing section in Chapter 5.)

5. **Oral presentations.** A final research project can take many forms, including written, visual, or oral. Although there are some similarities in the processes before this step, students need to be aware that oral presentations are often organized and presented in a different manner than written products. Many students with learning difficulties do not know how preparation and delivery of written and oral products differ. Many students may have the conception that an oral presentation means reading a written paper aloud. Therefore, guidelines should be given to these students so that they can easily adapt the information they have learned to an oral presentation. Provide students with the following guidelines for organizing their oral presentations:

   • Teach students to put important ideas from their notes or written product onto index cards. These ideas may not be full sentences, but phrases or words to help them remember key points.

- Teach students to number and color-code index cards to help organize their presentations.

- Require the use of visual or musical aids to enhance student presentations.

- Tell students that oral presentations are often less formal than written products, especially in the late elementary grades.

- Practice, practice, practice! It is very helpful for students to practice in front of a mirror so that they can see their style of presentation and learn their presentation.

Facilitate Homework Completion

Chronic failure to complete homework assignments should be a red flag to teachers. Failure to complete assignments may reflect problems at one of several levels, including:

- Poor organizational skills

- Difficulty comprehending instructions

- Difficulty comprehending the material

- Inability to handle the volume of material assigned

- Boredom with mundane or unchallenging assignments

It is critical for teachers to explore all the possible reasons why a student is not completing assignments. The strategies teachers, parents, and students will employ to remediate a homework problem will depend on the underlying cause of the difficulty.

You can facilitate homework completion using some of the techniques on the following page:

Techniques to Facilitate Homework Completion

❏ Require assignment notebooks.

❏ Monitor students' use of the notebooks.

❏ Allow a brief question-and-answer session at the end of class regarding homework.

❏ Provide an example of what is expected.

❏ Reduce the number of questions or problems for particular students when appropriate.

❏ Allow gifted students to complete challenging questions or projects.

❏ Start a homework club or extra help session at the end of the day.

❏ For long-term assignments, post reminders of due dates along the way and check students' progress.

❏ Schedule a parent–teacher–student conference if necessary.

Section III

Case Studies

Chapter 8

Selected Case Studies

••

Case Study, Jon   Age: 8½ years, Grade: 3

Jon, a bright 8½-year-old boy, was referred for evaluation in the third grade because of continuing reading problems. Jon's difficulties first became evident at the end of kindergarten when he failed to demonstrate knowledge of initial consonants. In the first grade, Jon's difficulty with sound–symbol correspondence continued. In the first and second grades, Jon received individual assistance in reading, but his skills showed little improvement and he continued to experience difficulties in reading as well as spelling.

Educational, cognitive, and linguistic testing was completed. Findings revealed a pattern of strengths and weaknesses consistent with the diagnosis of a learning disability and a mild attention deficit disorder. Specifically, Jon showed strengths in abstract reasoning, conceptualization, and the ability to memorize meaningful information related to context. Weaknesses were evident in spatial organization, spatial memory, automatic memory, and perceptual motor output. Jon also showed a high level of distractibility and impulsivity as the assessment tasks increased in difficulty.

In the reading area, Jon's learning disability manifested in problems with word attack and decoding skills, letter reversals, and poor sight vocabulary for isolated words. Although Jon knew some sound–symbol correspondence rules, he was inefficient in applying these rules when he blended words. Furthermore, his weak automatic memory limited his ability to read sight vocabulary. However, Jon's strong conceptual reasoning allowed him to use context clues to read text. Diagnostic teaching revealed that Jon was able to recognize, generalize, and apply linguistic patterns when these were taught in a structured and systematic fashion.

Spatial memory and motor weaknesses adversely affected Jon's writing skills. Because he was not automatic with alphabet production and had difficulties with motor planning and spatial organization, writing was a laborious process. The same processing difficulties that inhibited his reading were reflected in his poor spelling. Because of these specific difficulties, Jon's written output was limited and did not reflect his creativity and strong conceptual reasoning skills.

Jon's strengths in conceptual reasoning and problem solving were evident in the mathematics area, where he showed strengths in his math problem-solving skills. However, his performance was inefficient, and his computational accuracy was compromised by his weak memory for math facts and his inattentiveness to details.

As is evident from Table 8.1, recommendations emphasized the importance of instruction that would capitalize on Jon's conceptual strengths while incorporating a significant amount of time for revision, repetition, and review of previously learned material. It was recommended that Jon receive a structured phonetic approach to teach him sound–symbol correspondence rules and syllabication to improve his reading and spelling skills. Parallel instruction in reading and spelling was recommended to help Jon recognize the interrelationships between decoding (reading) and encoding (spelling). A process writing approach emphasizing successive revisions was suggested to build on Jon's conceptual reasoning strengths while addressing his specific spelling problems. In the math area, it was suggested that Jon be taught to automatize math facts and to focus on relevant details during the computation process. It was emphasized that Jon's attentional issues should be addressed in all content areas and that he develop independent work habits by generating personalized procedure and self-check lists.

Table 8.1. Case Study: Jon—Grade 3

Processing Areas	Educational Manifestations	Recommendations
STRENGTHS		
Conceptualizing information	Strong comprehension of linguistic information	*Reading* Prereading strategies: Activate prior knowledge. Use brainstorming. Use semantic mapping and webbing.
Reasoning and problem solving	Above average vocabulary skills	Use vocabulary splash. Set purposes for reading. Use active reading strategies. Encourage use of context cues.
Memorizing meaningful information in context		Model self-questioning. Use reciprocal teaching.
	Strong comprehension in content areas	Listen to literature read aloud by teachers, parents, audiotapes. *Writing* Process writing approach focusing on brainstorming, elaboration, and multiple edits. Teach story structure.
	Accurately analyzes and formulates solutions to math problems	*Math* Encourage estimation. Teach math skills in context of problem solving. Use manipulatives. Use reciprocal teaching. *(continued)*

Table 8.1. *Continued*

Processing Areas	Educational Manifestations	Recommendations
WEAKNESSES		
Automatic memory	Poor word attack/ decoding	Use an integrated language arts program, which maintains consistent approach to reading, writing, and spelling.
	Computational inaccuracy Weak memory for facts	Drill math facts (games, index cards, computer programs).
Spatial memory	Poor spelling	Use multisensory phonetic instruction with parallel presentation of decoding and encoding. Use supplemental linguistic instruction emphasizing word families and rhyming. Maintain individual word bank. Develop personal editing checklist.
Spatial organization	Poor handwriting	Introduce cursive writing and insure that Jon uses this consistently. *Individual classroom modifications* Teach cursive handwriting. Capitalize on computer technology, word processing, software for reading, and math drill.
Perceptual-motor output	Limited written output	Use a process writing approach that is structured and spiraled. Teach Jon to self-check using mnemonic strategies (e.g., COPS: Capitalization, Organization, Punctuation, Sentence structure and spelling).
Attention	Difficulty following multistep directions	Use preferential seating near teacher and/or away from distractions when necessary.
	Impulsive behavior Distractible, does not complete tasks	Break down multistep directions and repeat if necessary
	Inattentive to details	Develop individualized checklist for self-monitoring

....

Case Study, Lisa
Age: 9 years, Grade: 4

Lisa is a 9-year-old fourth-grade student who has had language, reading, and writing difficulties since kindergarten. She was evaluated during her first-grade year. Although she was diagnosed as gifted learning disabled with characteristics of attention deficit disorder with hyperactivity, she did not receive any special education services at that time. However, due to continued academic and social difficulties, Lisa had a complete speech and language evaluation at the end of her second-grade year. Test findings indicated deficits in auditory processing, receptive language, and expressive language. She began to work with a private educational specialist on a weekly basis. Due to her ongoing learning difficulties and frustration, behavioral problems began to occur within the classroom.

At the age of 9 years, Lisa was re-evaluated. Cognitive and educational testing indicated a diagnosis of a specific learning disability compounded by attentional weaknesses and social problems. Strengths were evident in the area of visual memory, as well as expression of ideas in writing. Weaknesses were evident in auditory memory, expressive language, phonological processing, planning, and organization.

In the academic areas, Lisa experienced delays of approximately 1 year in reading decoding and comprehension, spelling, handwriting, writing mechanics (capitalization and punctuation), and math word problems. In the reading area, her strengths in visual memory allowed her to read sight words easily; this improved her reading fluency. However, phonological processing weaknesses resulted in laborious decoding skills, and Lisa had difficulty sounding out grade-level word lists. She also had difficulty conceptualizing main themes and recalling details about a short narrative. This was attributed to her underlying weaknesses in auditory memory and her difficulties prioritizing information. Lisa's spelling skills were also 1 year below grade level. She had trouble when spelling multisyllabic words with long and short vowel sounds. In the writing area, Lisa's stories reflected many creative ideas and a strong imagination and included a beginning, middle, and end. She did not include capitals or punctuation. Her writing was difficult to read, as many of her letters were poorly formed.

As is evident from Table 8.2, it was recommended that Lisa receive educational therapy utilizing a systematic, structured, multisensory approach. This approach would capitalize on her visual strengths, but would also emphasize the specific strategies needed to improve her phonological awareness for spelling and decoding. It was suggested that Lisa explicitly learn the six syllable types and specific decoding rules, as well as finger-spelling techniques, which emphasize phonological segmentation.

As a result of this individualized support and other recommendations, Lisa has made great progress. Behavior within the classroom has improved as her academic frustration has decreased. Medication has helped to control her attention deficit disorder, and she is less impulsive and more thoughtful with her work. Lisa is now performing well in her classes, and she has a more positive self-esteem.

Table 8.2. Case Study: Lisa—Grade 4

Processing Areas	Educational Manifestations	Recommendations
STRENGTHS		
Receptive language	Uses mature vocabulary while writing and speaking	Prewriting—brainstorm lists of words.
Creative ideas for written expression	Imaginative and creative ideas in writing	Write for content first. Separate grades for content and mechanics.
Visual memory	Good at reading sight words	Further develop sight vocabulary based on critical concepts in class.
WEAKNESSES		
Auditory memory	May not recall information presented orally. Trouble following multistep oral directions	Needs both written and oral directions.
Expressive language	Slow and imprecise when responding in class	Alert Lisa in advance of being called on so she has time to formulate her oral responses. Use semantic mapping and outlining for prewriting.
Phonological processing	Difficulty decoding. Difficulty analyzing words. Difficulty spelling	Use multisensory approach including instruction in syllable types and specific decoding rules. Use finger-spelling.
Organization of language	May not recall information obtained through reading. Difficulty conceptualizing main themes and recalling details about narratives and text	Teach a structured, systematic, multisensory approach to reading comprehension. Teach visualization and chunking strategies. Use reciprocal teaching.

Case Study, Maria

Age: 12 years, Grade: 6

Maria is a 12-year-old sixth grader who was referred for an evaluation because of her failure to complete classwork and homework and her poor test performance. Her teachers reported that she is extremely distractible in class and that she disrupts others. These problems were first noted in kindergarten and have continued through the years. A number of trials of stimulant medication therapy have been initiated in the past with little success.

The assessment included educational, cognitive, and linguistic testing, as well as a review of Maria's developmental history. Findings were consistent with the diagnosis of an attention deficit disorder with hyperactivity. Maria demonstrated strengths in verbal and nonverbal problem-solving and reasoning abilities. Short-term memory skills were strong.

Weaknesses were evident in automatic memory and long-term memory. Maria also used poor self-monitoring abilities and showed limited attention to details. Organizational difficulties occurred frequently. Some areas of language were also weak, including word-retrieval skills, vocabulary knowledge, and the understanding of inferential and metaphoric language. However, when language was more literal, receptive and expressive language skills were age-appropriate.

Educational testing indicated that Maria had acquired grade-appropriate academic skills. In the area of reading, Maria displayed grade-appropriate skills in word recognition, decoding, and general comprehension. However, poor attention contributed to her difficulty in keeping her place while reading, and she often skipped over words or lines. In addition, she had difficulty with vocabulary. In the area of writing, Maria's strengths in abstract reasoning were reflected in her ability to generate creative and meaningful themes. Attentional weaknesses contributed to her difficulties prioritizing and to her inconsistent use of punctuation, sentence structure, and spelling. In the area of math, Maria exhibited a good understanding of concepts and word problems, consistent with her strong reasoning abilities. Weak automatic memory was reflected in her hesitation with math facts. She made many errors typical of students with attention deficit disorders, including computational errors when she computed multistep calculations, poor self-monitoring, and inattention to details (e.g., decimals, dollar signs).

Maria's attention deficit disorder also manifested in the social area. Maria had difficulty establishing and maintaining friendships, in part due to her difficulties inhibiting her comments. She was seldom able to anticipate the consequences of her behavior. As a result, her self-confidence was diminished. She made many negative comments about herself and her work. She described many worries and reportedly exhibited somatic signs of tension (e.g., frequent headaches, nail-biting).

As is evident from Table 8.3, it was recommended that Maria receive numerous classroom modifications to accommodate her attention deficit disorder so that she could begin to experience success. Educational therapy services were recommended to help her develop effective educational strategies. Psychotherapy was also recommended to address social-emotional issues. Specific recommendations are outlined in the table.

Table 8.3. Case Study: Maria—Grade 6

Processing Areas	Educational Manifestations	Recommendations
STRENGTHS		
Abstract reasoning	Good understanding of concepts	Preview concepts at the beginning of each lesson or unit of study.
	Good overall reading and language comprehension	Teach prereading and prewriting strategies.
	Good math problem-solving ability	Relate new information to that which is known.
		Present information in meaningful contexts.
		Keep class discussions lively and relevant.
		Include hands-on, experiential projects and visual aids whenever possible.
Short-term memory	May grasp concepts initially but forget important facts and details over time	Teach recall strategies emphasizing mnemonics cues (e.g., acronyms, visual associations).
WEAKNESSES		
Automatic memory	Hesitates on math facts	Determine which memory facts are "stratofacts" or "clueless facts."
		Develop strategies for clueless facts before building up speed.
		Encourage use of computer games with appropriate facts at home or at school.
Long-term memory	Due to retrieval difficulties, may have problems accessing prior knowledge	Activate prior knowledge through brainstorming and discussion.
Attention	Distracted by external and internal stimuli	Use preferential seating.
	Inattentive during lecture	Develop a behavioral checklist targeting 45 key behaviors each day.
	Talks in class	
	Disrupts other students	
	Rarely participates	Set goals for daily and weekly performance.
Self-monitoring	Inconsistent use of punctuation, sentence structure, and spelling	Model the use of active strategies and self-instructions while performing complex math and writing assignments.
	Calculation errors in math, does not check her work or include details (e.g., decimals, dollar signs), confuses operational signs	Develop checklists for solving math processes or editing written work (e.g., FOIL, COPS).

(continued)

Table 8.3. *Continued*

Processing Areas	Educational Manifestations	Recommendations
	Loses her place in reading when comprehension falters (e.g., skips words, lines)	Teach active reading strategies, especially clarifying and self-questioning.
Organization	Forgets to bring assignments and materials to and from school	Have all assignments recorded in an assignment notebook, which is signed by teacher and parent. Develop a notebook/folder system for storing completed or assigned work papers. Develop a system for cross-checking materials going to and from school (e.g., peer assistance, use of icons).
	Has difficulty completing long-range assignments	Break the assignment into manageable units. Develop a study plan with goals and time lines. Check at various points along the process.
	Messy work space	Provide assistance with organization of locker at school and work space at home. Allow a few minutes each day for reorganization. Encourage parents to do the same for work space at home.
	Difficulty prioritizing ideas	Teach organizational strategies for reading and writing, including semantic mapping, two-column note taking, pre-writing strategies.
Vocabulary knowledge	Misses key information when reading	Preview vocabulary before a lesson or unit of study. Develop a personalized word bank. Teach recall strategies (e.g., key word) and structural properties. Teach strategies for analyzing word meanings through context.

Case Study, Sam   Age: 14 years, Grade: 8

Sam is a 14-year-old eighth grader who has been experiencing considerable difficulty with reading and writing. Sam's problems were evident from an early age, and special needs services were provided. However, little progress was made. At the age of 9 years, an evaluation resulted in the diagnosis of a learning disability and recommendations for intensive remediation. At age 10, Sam began to exhibit behavior problems, including aggressive behaviors and difficulty with peers. Sam's lack of progress led to diminished self-confidence, and he showed a pattern of "learned helplessness." He demonstrated limited motivation and had considerable difficulty completing tasks, thus falling further behind. He began to socialize with a "tough" crowd at school and exhibited numerous discipline problems.

At age 13, Sam was re-evaluated. Educational, cognitive, and linguistic testing confirmed the diagnosis of a language-based learning disability. Sam demonstrated strengths in his reasoning ability, range of knowledge, understanding of part–whole relationships, and visual memory. He performed best on tasks that provided an overt structure. Weaknesses were evident in the areas of receptive and expressive language, auditory processing skills, organization, fine-motor skills, and phonological awareness.

In academic areas, Sam demonstrated relative strengths in the area of math, with his performance falling solidly in the average range. It appeared that Sam's strong reasoning abilities and understanding of part–whole relationships contributed to his success with math. He also benefited from the highly structured nature of mathematical processes. In the area of reading, Sam demonstrated variable performance in decoding skills. Although gains had been made over the years, he still made many errors and lacked automaticity. Sam's reading comprehension was also variable. He showed strengths on tasks that capitalized on reasoning abilities and minimized memory. He showed weaknesses on tasks that required organization of verbal material and integration of details. In the area of writing, Sam's fine-motor weaknesses made writing a slow, arduous process. Spelling skills were problematic, due to his weaknesses in phonological awareness. Sam's written expression lacked thematic continuity due to problems with language and organization. Additional language weaknesses were reflected in his use of simple sentence structures and immature vocabulary.

A wide range of educational recommendations were introduced for Sam (see Table 8.4). Since he began to receive intensive remediation and classroom modifications, he has begun to make significant strides in his academic work. His academic successes have motivated him to become a more active participant in the learning process. This increased motivation has fostered a positive attitude and improved self-confidence. His behavior has also improved, and he rarely gets into trouble. He is presently alert and attentive in class, and completes his work on time.

Table 8.4. Case Study: Sam—Grade 8

Processing Areas	Educational Manifestations	Recommendations
STRENGTHS		
Verbal and nonverbal reasoning	Understands complex math concepts when these are presented in a structured way	When introducing a new math concept, develop the concept through use of manipulatives and/or visual representations *before* presenting the computational process.
Understanding of part–whole relationships	Benefits from instructional strategies with visual-spatial features	Use graphic organizers/ semantic mapping when introducing language concepts, including content area information.
Visual memory	Understands and remembers best when information is presented visually	Teach recall strategies that emphasize visual features (e.g., imagery, visual associations). Use visual aids whenever possible.
Range of knowledge	Has a wide variety of experience and knowledge of the world around him	Engage in prereading and prewriting activities to activate prior knowledge and set purposes for reading. Record these ideas on a semantic map and integrate with new information.
WEAKNESSES		
Receptive and expressive language	Often misinterprets directions Poor reading comprehension Limited written output, simple sentence structure	Check with him periodically to insure that he has grasped the directions. Encourage him to request help when needed and to decrease his dependence on teacher-initiated checks. Use process writing approaches. Use vocabulary building strategies. Use prereading and prewriting strategies to emphasize vocabulary and language enrichment. Use semantic mapping for prewriting.
Auditory memory	Weak spelling skills	Teach Sam spelling rules. Use mnemonics for checking his spelling. Use individualized spelling checklists.
Fine-motor skills	Writing slow and labored	Encourage Sam to use a word processor to bypass the writing task.

Case Study, Amy

Age: 15 years, Grade: 9

Amy is a 15-year-old high school student who is motivated and works hard in every class. Despite her effort and positive attitude toward school, Amy has earned low grades in every subject except mathematics. Her teachers reported that she has had problems with reading rate, comprehension, and vocabulary. Amy's struggles with reading first began in the first grade. An evaluation showed that Amy had a 40-point discrepancy between her verbal and performance scores on the WISC-R. In elementary school, Amy received intermittent special education services in reading and speech. Currently, Amy is being tutored in history by an older student. Educational, cognitive, and linguistic testing confirmed the presence of a language-based learning disability.

Results of the assessment indicated Amy's very weak receptive and expressive language skills. In particular, her vocabulary and her use of syntax were poorly developed. Consequently, although she may have understood concepts, she did not communicate effectively in tests or papers. Writing papers was especially difficult for Amy, because she was required to organize and rephrase material she had not fully comprehended. Amy also exhibited weaknesses in auditory memory and problems with information retrieval. Because of her auditory memory weaknesses, Amy did not retain information consistently. Her reading was slow and her comprehension weak. Amy displayed numerous strengths in visual-perceptual functioning, nonverbal reasoning, and memory. These strengths were apparent in math.

As is evident from Table 8.5, it was recommended that Amy learn strategies to enhance her reading comprehension and retention of material. It was also suggested that she be taught strategies for organizing and monitoring her written work.

Table 8.5. Case Study: Amy—Grade 9

Processing Areas	Educational Manifestations	Recommendations
STRENGTHS		
Nonverbal reasoning	Readily and accurately completes mathematics problems	Provide classroom accommodations. Provide visual supports for lecture classes.
Visual memory	Retains information more easily when it is presented visually	Photocopy notes. Allow untimed tests.
WEAKNESSES		
Auditory memory	Spends time studying but does not retain the material May not consistently recall information presented in lecture format	*Reading* Link new information with previous knowledge. Contextualize to help with meaning.
Receptive language and vocabulary	Has difficulty deriving meaning from written or spoken language	View a film before reading. Use active reading strategies.
	Struggles to understand concepts presented auditorially	Use semantic mapping and webbing. Use highlighters: blue = main idea, red = details. Use margin notes.
	Has difficulty drawing inferences May miss metaphoric expressions	Use Skim, Rap, and Map. Use two-column notes. Draw pictures of metaphoric expressions. Use imagery.
Expressive language and word retrieval	Problems writing papers Slow and imprecise when responding orally in the classroom	*Vocabulary* Use VOCAB-LIT with drawings. Use key words. *Writing* Prewriting—Make authority inventory. Use semantic mapping. Use revision strategies: color code, peer work.

Appendixes

Appendix 1

Graph for Estimating Readability—Extended

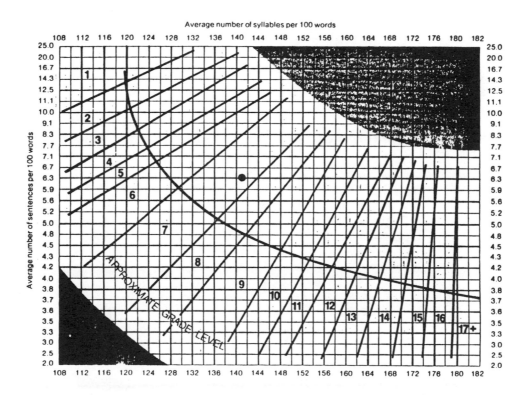

Note. From *The Reading Teacher's Book of Lists* (2nd ed., p. 365), by B. L. Fry, J. E. Kress, and D. L. Fountoukidis, 1993, Englewood, NJ: Prentice Hall. Reprinted with permission.

Strategies Used in Reciprocal Teaching

Summarizing

Requires students to identify, paraphrase, and integrate the most important information in a text

Can be done on various levels (sentence, paragraph, passage)

Clarifying

Requires students to know when they don't know and to take the necessary steps to restore the meaning

Question-Generating

Requires students to identify significant information, generate a question about it, listen to peer responses, and be able to answer question

Predicting

Requires students to hypothesize what the author will discuss next

Develops understanding of headings, subheadings, etc.

Appendix 2b

Implementing Reciprocal Teaching

1. Discuss with students purposes for reciprocal teaching.

   - Discuss why text may be difficult to understand.

   - Discuss why it is important to have strategies.

   - Discuss how the reciprocal teaching procedure will assist students to understand and monitor what they read.

2. Give an overall description of the procedure, including the following:

   - Have a dialogue/discussion about text.

   - Describe turn-taking for teacher/leader.

   - Describe "duties" of teacher/leader with respect to strategies.

3. Introduce each of the four strategies separately, only one each day.

   - Start with easy content (favorite movie, class activity).

   - Advance to short paragraphs with simple main ideas.

   - Then, use more complex paragraphs containing redundant and trivial information.

4. Begin the dialogue.

   - Teacher initiates and sustains dialogue for first few days to present a good model.

   - Start with single paragraphs from well-organized texts.

Note. From "Reciprocal Teaching: Can Student Discussions Boost Comprehension?" by A. S. Palincsar, 1987, *Instructor,* 56–60. Adapted with permission.

5. As students acquire more practice, teacher shifts from "teacher" to "coach," imparting more responsibility to and prompting more participation from students.

- Teacher adjusts feedback/level of involvement to individual needs of students.

- Less capable students may require more assistance and modeling.

- More capable students become new models.

- All students participate but at their appropriate levels.

Venn Diagram for Comparison/Contrast

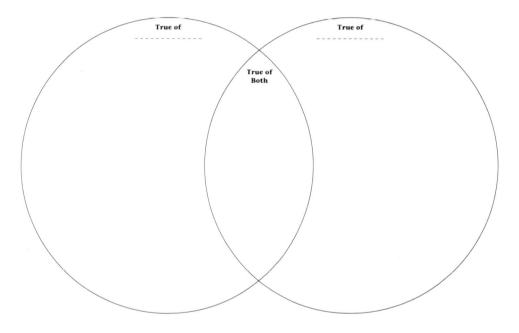

Appendix 4

Mining for Topics

- Who are the special people in your life? Mom, Dad, Grandmother, Grandfather? Brother? Sister, Uncle? Other? Write them down.

- Are there special things you do together? List them.

- Special places that you go? Family fun that you remember?

- What are some of the things that excite you about your family?

- Do you have a special friend? What do you do together?

- What do you like to do in your spare time? Favorite games? Hobbies? Collections?

- Have you ever taken a really great trip? Did something funny happen? Something scary? Something exciting?

- Have you ever seen anything unusual?

- What is the funniest thing that ever happened to you?

- Do you remember a time when your feelings were really hurt? When you were embarrassed?

- What makes you sad? Afraid? Very glad? Laugh?

- Have you ever been really lonely, with no one to play with?

- What are some of the things that bug you?

- Do you have a pet? More than one? How do you care for your pet? Have you ever lost a pet?

- What are you very good at? Some kids are good at a sport. Some are very good at drawing or making people laugh. Some are very good at being kind and thoughtful.

Note. Developed and adapted by Jacqueline Finn, educational consultant, Worcester, MA.

- Think of something you do very well.

- What are your favorite foods? Favorite possessions?

- Do you have a special place that you like to go to by yourself? Some kids like to lie on pillows in their closets. Some like to sit or lie on large rocks.

- Do you know a lot about something: Skateboarding? Riding a scooter? Bike tricks? Tools, cars? Books? People? Cooking?

- What is the best thing about school? The worst?

- Are there some holidays that you celebrate in special ways? Birthdays?

Glossary

active reading: The process of reading a text so that a person monitors his or her understanding.

attention deficit disorder (ADD): A disorder that involves a significant amount of impulsivity, distractibility, and inattention. Attention deficit disorder with hyperactivity (ADHD) includes an additional component of excessive motor activity or restlessness.

automatic memory: The part of memory that allows a person to recall unrelated, rote information immediately. An example is recalling math facts quickly.

cloze procedures: A technique used in testing and teaching reading comprehension in which words are omitted in a passage and the student is asked to insert words that complete the sentence.

decoding: The process of relating written letters with specific sounds and blending sounds to form words.

diagnostic teaching: A series of trial lessons or teaching probes that are used to determine the optimal teaching method for a student while simultaneously continuing to assess that student's strengths and weaknesses.

explicit instruction: Teaching a concept directly in a systematic and structured manner.

learned helplessness: A state of mind in which a person has repeatedly failed and believes he or she can succeed only by relying on others for assistance.

learning disability: A discrepancy between a student's average to above average intellectual ability and low level of academic performance in different aspects of learning, specifically listening, speaking, reading, writing, and math.

learning style: A student's unique profile of strengths and weaknesses in processing and academic areas.

mnemonic devices: Methods that help individuals learn and memorize by making unrelated material meaningful, familiar, and more accessible; for example, making a word from the first letters of a list.

multisensory approaches: Teaching methods that utilize several sensory modalities. An example is learning a new word by hearing, seeing, touching, drawing, and saying it.

phonological awareness: The knowledge that words can be auditorially segmented into individual sounds or segments, a process necessary for decoding and spelling skills. For example, the word *shut* can be broken into three sounds: /sh/, /u/, and /t/.

process-oriented assessment: Diagnostic testing that focuses on how a student learns.

processing (e.g., language, auditory, visual): The manner in which information is taken in through the different senses, manipulated, and transformed into meaningful, accessible knowledge. A deficit in a processing area can lead to specific difficulties in academic areas. For example, an auditory processing deficit can interfere with a child's reading development.

readability index: A procedure for calculating the approximate grade level of a written text.

reading comprehension: The process of gaining meaning from written text.

recall tests: Teacher-made tests that require students to recall specific answers within a given context. Question types include fill-in-the-blank, listing, diagramming, and labeling.

recognition tests: Teacher-made tests that require students to recognize the correct response. Question types include multiple choice, true/false and matching.

self-esteem: The positive or negative view a person has about himself or herself.

self-monitoring: The process of independent self-checking in all subject areas. For example, in reading, self-monitoring may include self-questioning to insure comprehension of text; in math, self-monitoring may involve checking for computational errors.

semantic mapping: A graphic representation of the relationships between the meanings of words and ideas. Mapping can be used as a prereading, postreading, prewriting, and/or organizational strategy.

spiral instruction: A method of teaching that emphasizes systematic repetition and review.

strategy: A specific procedure for accomplishing tasks that can help students improve their problem-solving, reading, writing, and math performance.

visual-spatial organization: The arrangement of objects or symbols in space, in isolation, and in relation to others.

visualization: A method that helps a person create a picture of an idea or object in his or her mind. This method is often used to help students with spelling and reading comprehension weaknesses.

word-retrieval difficulty: A language- and memory-based difficulty in which a person has trouble recalling specific words, names, or labels, even though the word may be part of his or her vocabulary.

Recommended Reading

Books and Articles About Learning Disabilities and Strategy Use

Choate, J. S. (1993). *Successful mainstreaming: Proven ways to detect and correct special needs.* Boston: Allyn & Bacon.

Gaskins, E., & Elliot, T. (1991). *Implementing cognitive strategy training across the school.* Cambridge, MA: Brookline.

Levine, M. (1993). *All kinds of minds.* Cambridge, MA: EPS. (for students and teachers).

Levine, M. (1990). *Keeping a head in school.* Cambridge, MA: EPS. (for students and teachers).

Mastropieri, M. A., & Scruggs, T. E. (1988). Increasing the content area learning of learning disabled students: Research implementation. *Learning Disabilities Research 4,* 17–25.

Mastropieri, M. A., & Scruggs, T. (1991). *Teaching students ways to remember: Strategies for learning mnemonically.* Cambridge, MA: Brookline.

Meltzer, L. J. (Ed.). (1993). *Strategy assessment and instruction for students with learning disabilities: From theory to practice.* Austin, TX: PRO-ED.

Meltzer, L. J., & Solomon, B. (1988). *Educational prescriptions for the classroom for students with learning problems.* Cambridge, MA: Educators Publishing Service.

Pressley, M., & Associates. (1995). *Cognitive strategy instruction that really improves children's academic performance* (2nd ed.). Cambridge, MA: Brookline.

Books About Attention Deficit Disorder

Alexander-Roberts, C. (1994). *The ADHD parenting handbook.* Dallas: Taylor.

Barkley, R. A. (1990). *Attention deficit hyperactivity disorder: A handbook for diagnosis and treatment.* New York: Guilford.

Hallowell, E. M., & Ratey, J. J. (1994). *Driven to distraction.* New York: Pantheon.

McNamara, B., & McNamara, F. (1994). *Keys to parenting a child with ADD.* New York: Barrons.

Umansky, W., & Smalley, B. (1994). *ADD: Helping your child to untie the knot of attention deficit disorders.* New York: Warner.

Wender, P. H. (1987). *The hyperactive child, adolescent and adult: Attention deficit disorder through the lifespan.* Oxford: Oxford University Press.

Books and Articles About Strategies in Specific Areas

Bley, N. S., & Thornton, C. A. (1989). *Teaching mathematics to the learning disabled.* Austin, TX: PRO-ED.

Clark, D. B. (1988). *Dyslexia: Theory and practice of remedial instruction.* Parkton, MD: York.

Dupuis, M. M. (Ed.). (1984). *Reading in the content areas: Research for teachers.* Newark, NJ: IRA.

Harris, K. R., & Graham, S. (1992). *Helping young writers master the craft: Strategy instruction and self-regulation in the writing process.* Cambridge, MA: Brookline.

Meltzer, L. J. (1993). *Strategy assessment and instruction for students with learning disabilities: From theory to practice.* Austin, TX: PRO-ED.

Montague, M. (1985). Teaching verbal mathematical problem solving skills to students. In C. Simon (Ed.), *Communication skills and classroom success: Therapy methodologies for language-learning disabled students* (pp. 365–377). San Diego: College-Hill.

Tierney, R. J., Readence, J. E., & Deshner, E. K. (1985). *Reading strategies and practice: A compendium* (2nd ed.). Boston: Allyn & Bacon.

Zorfass, J., Corley, P., Remz, A., & Ethier, D. (1994). Promoting technology in special education: Supporting change agents. *Technology and Disability, 3*(2), 158–164.

Books About the Social Aspects of Learning Disabilities

Brooks, R. (1991). *The self-esteem teacher.* Circle Pines, MN: American Guidance Service.

Osman, B. B. (1982). *No one to play with: The social side of learning disabilities.* Novato, CA: Academic Therapy.

Osman, B. B. (1987). Promoting social acceptance of children with learning disabilities. *Journal of Reading, Writing and Learning Disabilities International, 3*(2), 111–119.

Vaughn, S., Schumm, J., & Kouzekanani, K. (1993). What do students with learning disabilities think when their general education teachers make adaptations? *Journal of Learning Disabilities, 26*(8), 545–555.

References

Anders, P. L., Bos, C., & Filip, D. (1984). *The effect of semantic feature analysis on the reading comprehension of learning disabled students.* Paper presented at the Annual Meeting of the National Reading Association. (ERIC Document Reproduction Service No. ED 237 969)

Atwell, N. (1987). *In the middle: Writing, reading, and learning with adolescents.* Portsmouth, NH: Heinemann.

Bell, N. (1991). *Visualizing and verbalizing: For language comprehension and thinking.* Paso Robles, CA: Academy of Reading.

Brown, A. L., & Campione, J. C. (1986). Psychological theory and the study of learning disabilities. *American Psychologist, 41,* 1059–1068.

Butler, A. (1988). *Guided reading.* Crystal Lake, IL: Rigby.

Byars, B. (1989). *Trouble river.* New York: Puffin.

Chall, J. S. (1983). *Stages of reading development.* New York: McGraw-Hill

Chall, J. S. (1987). Two vocabularies for reading: Recognition and meaning. In M. G. McKeown & M. E. Curtis (Eds.), *The nature of vocabulary acquisition* (pp. 7–17). Hillsdale, NH: Erlbaum.

Chase, A., & Duffelmeyer, F. (1990). VOCAB-LIT: Integrating vocabulary study and literature study. *Journal of Reading, 34*(3), 188–193.

Ciborowski, J. (1992). *Textbooks and the student who can't read them.* Cambridge, MA: Brookline Books.

Coburn, T. G., Hoogeboom, S., & Goodnow, J. (1989). *The problem solver with calculators.* Mountain View, CA: Creative Publications.

Curtis, M. E. (1986). The best kind of vocabulary instruction. *Massachusetts Primer, 15,* 5–9.

Curtis, M. E. (1987). Vocabulary testing and vocabulary instruction. In M. G. McKeown & M. E. Curtis (Eds.), *The nature of vocabulary acquisition* (pp. 37–51). Hillsdale, NJ: Erlbaum.

Deshler, D. D., & Schumaker, J. B. (1986). Learning strategies: An instructional alternative for low achieving adolescents. *Exceptional Children, 52*(6), 583–590.

Durkin, D. (1976). *Teaching word identification.* Boston: Allyn & Bacon.

Endsley, M. (1991). *Eastern hemisphere.* Oakland, NJ: Scott Foresman.

Englert, C. S. (1992). Writing instruction from a sociocultural perspective: The holistic, dialogic, and social enterprise of writing. *Journal of Learning Disabilities, 25*(3), 153–172.

Garner, R. (1987). *Metacognition and reading comprehension.* Norwood, NJ: Ablex.

Garner, R., Hare, V., Alexander, P., Haynes, J., & Winograd, P. (1984). Inducing use of a text lookback strategy among unsuccessful readers. *American Educational Research Journal, 21,* 789–798.

Graham, L., & Wong, B. (1993). Comparing two modes of teaching a question-answering strategy for enhancing reading comprehension: Didactic and self-instruction training. *Journal of Learning Disabilities, 26,* 270–279.

Greene, V., & Enfield, M. (1986). *Project Read: Phonology guide*. Bloomington, IN: Language Circle Enterprise.

Harris, K., & Graham, S. (1992). *Helping young writers master the craft: Strategy instruction and self-regulation in the writing process*. Cambridge, MA: Brookline.

Hasselbring, T., Goin, L., & Bransford, J. (1988). Developing math automaticity in learning handicapped children: The role of computerized drill and practice. *Teaching Exceptional Children, 20*(6), 3–7.

Hillocks, G. (1986). *Research on written composition: New directions for teaching*. Urbana, IL: Clearinghouse on Reading and Communication Skills and the National Conference on Research in English.

Indrisano, R. (1984). Reading and writing revisited. *Ginn Occasional Papers*. Columbus, OH: Ginn.

Johnson, D. (n.d.). Three sound strategies for vocabulary development. *Ginn Occasional Papers No. 3*. Columbus, OH: Ginn.

Kaplan, E., & Tuchman, A. (1985). *Vocabulary strategies*. Madison: Wisconsin Center for Educational Research, NIE. (ERIC Document Reproduction Service No. ED 262 380)

Kintsch, W., & Van Dijk, T. (1978). Toward a model of text comprehension and production. *Psychological Review, 85*, 363–394.

Licht, B. (1993). Achievement-related beliefs in children with learning disabilities: Impact on motivation and strategic learning. In L. J. Meltzer (Ed.), *Strategy assessment and instruction for students with learning disabilities: From theory to practice* (pp. 195–220). Austin, TX: PRO-ED.

Lindamood, C., & Lindamood, P. (1975). *Auditory Discrimination in Depth*. Austin, TX: PRO-ED.

Mastropieri, M., Scruggs, T., & Levin, J. (1985). Maximizing what exceptional children can learn: A review of research on the keyword method and related mnemonic techniques. *Remedial and Special Education, 6*(2), 39–45.

Meltzer, L. J. (1993a). Strategy use in children with learning disabilities: The challenge of assessment. In L. J. Meltzer (Ed.), *Strategy assessment and instruction for students with learning disabilities: From theory to practice* (pp. 93–136). Austin, TX: PRO-ED.

Meltzer, L. J. (1993b). Assessment of learning disabilities: The challenge of evaluating the cognitive strategies and processes underlying learning. In G. R. Lyon (Ed.), *Frames of reference for the assessment of learning disabilities* (pp. 571–606). Baltimore, MD: Brookes.

Meltzer, L. J. (1993c, October). *Are LD students' self perceptions of their academic strategies and competence realistic?* Paper presented at the International Academy for Research in Learning Disabilities, Boston.

Meltzer, L. J. (in press). Strategic learning in LD students: The role of students' self-awareness and self-perceptions. In T. Scruggs & M. Mastropieri (Eds.), *Advances in learning and behavioral disabilities*. Greenwich, CT: JAI Press.

Meltzer, L. J., & Roditi, B. (in press). *The student observation system (S.O.S.)*. ResearchILD.

Miller, S. P., & Mercer, C. D. (1993). Mneumonics: Enhancing the math performance of students with learning difficulties. *Intervention in School and Clinic, 29*(2), 78–82.

Murray, D. (1984). *Write to learn*. New York: Holt, Rinehart & Winston.

Nagy, W., Herman, P., & Anderson, R. (1985). Learning words from context. *Reading Research Quarterly, 20*, 233–253.

O'Rourke, J. (1974). *Toward a science of vocabulary development*. The Hague, The Netherlands: Mouton.

Orton, J. (1966). The Orton-Gillingham approach. In J. Money (Ed.), *The disabled reader* (pp. 119–146). Baltimore: The Johns Hopkins University Press.

Palincsar, A. S. (1987, January). Reciprocal teaching: Can student discussions boost comprehension? *Instructor*, 56–60.

Paris, S. G., & Winograd, P. (1990). How metacognition can promote academic learning and instruction. In B. Jones & L. Idol (Eds.), *Dimensions of thinking and cognitive instruction*. Hillsdale, NJ: Erlbaum.

Pearson, P. (1984). Asking questions about stories. In A. Harris & E. Sipay (Eds.), *Readings on reading instruction* (pp. 274–283). White Plains, NY: Longman.

Pressley, M. (1988). Can learning disabled students become good information processors? How can we find out? In L. V. Feagans, G. J. Short, & L. J. Meltzer (Eds.), *Subtypes of learning disabilities: Theoretical perspectives and research* (pp. 137–161). Hillsdale, NJ: Erlbaum.

Pressley, M., Goodchild, F., Fleet, J., Zajchowski, R., & Evans, E. D. (1989). The challenges of classroom strategy instruction. *Elementary School Journal, 89,* 301–342.

Pressley, M., & Harris, K. (1990). What we really know about strategy instruction. *Educational Leadership,* September, 31–34.

Putnam, M. L., Deshler, D. D., & Schumaker, J. B. (1993). The investigation of setting demands: A missing link in learning strategy instruction. In L. Meltzer (Ed.), *Strategy assessment and instruction for students with learning disabilities* (pp. 325–353). Austin, TX: PRO-ED.

Raphael, T., & Gavelek, J. (1984). Question-related activities and their relationship to reading comprehension: Some instructional implications. In G. Duffy, L. Roehler, & J. Mason (Eds.), *Comprehension instruction: Perspectives and suggestions* (pp. 234–250). New York: Longman.

Rhodes, L. K., & Dudley-Marling, C. (1988). *Readers and writers with a difference.* Portsmouth, NH: Heinemann.

Roditi, B. (1993). Mathematics assessment and strategy instruction: An applied developmental approach. In L. J. Meltzer (Ed.), *Strategy assessment and instruction for students with learning disabilities: From theory to practice* (pp. 293–324). Austin, TX: PRO-ED.

Roswell, F. G., & Natchez, G. (1977). *Reading disability.* New York: Basic Books.

Squire, J. (1984). Composing and comprehending: Two sides of the same basic process. In J. M. Jensen (Ed.), *Composing and comprehending* (pp. 23–30). Urbana, IL: NCTE.

Stanovich, K. (1986). Matthew effects in reading: Some consequences of individual differences in the acquisition of literacy. *Reading Research Quarterly, 21,* 360–407.

Swanson, H. L. (1991). *Handbook on the assessment of learning disabilities: Theory, research, and practice.* Austin, TX: PRO-ED.

Wilson, B. (1988). *Wilson reading system.* Millbury, MA: Wilson Language Training.

Wilson, B. (1992). *Wilson Success System: Study and writing skills program.* Millbury, MA: Wilson Language Training.

Wolf, D. P., LeMahieu, P. G., & Eresh, J. (1992). Good measure: Assessment as a tool for educational reform. *Educational Leadership, 49,* 8–13.

Wolf, M., & Dickinson, D. (1985). From oral to written language: Transitions in the school years. In J. Gleason (Ed.), *The development of language* (pp. 227–276). Columbus, OH: Merrill.